MW00618441

Beyond Denial

Why Addicts Relapse

by

Patrick Caffrey, LPC

Second Edition

Paraclete Counseling Center Press

Paraclete Counseling Center Press
Suwanee, GA
http://www.paracletecounseling.com

ISBN 978-0-615-36737-8

Neither do I condemn thee.

John 8:11

Table of Contents

Introduction

The treatment of addiction comes in all shapes and sizes, and considering the diversity, it may surprise us that the popular disease concept and the medical model are such recent arrivals on the scene. It's only since 1956 that the medical people have climbed aboard the bandwagon which shouldn't be confused with the wagon that reformed drunks are sometimes said to be riding.

Of course, people have been treating addicts, especially alcoholics for much longer than half a century. In fact the treatment of alcoholics has been going on for thousands of years. Unfortunately, most of the effort has focused on treating them as moral degenerates, weaklings, parasites, social outcasts, antisocial personalities, sociopaths, psychopaths, and common criminals. As a group, persons suffering from addiction were more likely to wind up in jail than in hospitals.

We've come a long way, baby, in the half century since the American Medical Association declared alcoholism to be a disease. A little earlier than that, Bill Wilson and company gave birth to Alcoholics Anonymous which marked the beginning of the first relatively successful attempt to address the problem while acknowledging the inherent value and dignity of persons who suffer from addiction. Of course, that acknowledgement didn't erase the stigma. To this day, the name Alcoholics *Anonymous* continues to speak to a wish for concealment (a kind of denial, perhaps) and every addictions counselor is familiar with individuals and their families who travel to remote towns and cities to seek help rather than risk being recognized by their neighbors.

But the purpose of this book is not to harangue the public about its attitudes toward addicts. In fact, although certain problems do exist in that vein, and even though an air of intolerance might be seen as a relapse factor for some recovering alcoholics, public opinion is the least of their problems. What is troubling is the fact that despite the availability of numerous treatment formats which are readily accessible in most locations, it is estimated that a relatively small percentage receive help and an equally small percentage of those receiving help manage to avoid relapse.

It's impossible to count those suffering from addiction, but considering alcohol alone, it's been estimated that 70 percent of Americans over the age of 14 drink, and a conservative estimate is that one in ten persons who drink is or will become alcoholic. Today, probably no more than one out of ten alcoholics seeks and receives treatment. Finally, 90 percent of those receiving treatment relapse within one year.

Historically there seem always to have been fringe groups who have taken the prohibition approach to the problem of addiction. However, attempts to label certain addictive substances as evil and persons who use them as sinners has met with negligible effectiveness as we examine the broader picture. Moreover, it is difficult to override the evidence that alcohol consumption is an innocuous social custom among a sizeable majority of the population.

We have alluded to a diversity of treatments available today. But what varies is the intensity and the extensiveness of treatment formats. There is little or no difference in the fundamental content of the programs offered. Specifically, all treatment approaches share the same goal, which is to break down the denial of the addict which manifests itself in avoidance of treatment and a refusal to stop drinking. When we evaluate treatment according to this benchmark, the majority of programs appear successful. Still, there's that annoying relapse figure.

Moving from lesser to greater on the scale of intensity of treatment we encounter Alcoholics Anonymous and other support groups. We move through outpatient counseling, intensive outpatient counseling, partial hospitalization, and both short and long term residential treatment. There are halfway houses and wilderness programs; secular and faith based programs; programs for adolescents and adults; programs for men; programs for women; and programs for men and women. There are programs overseen by medical personnel while others are led by pastoral counselors or those with a mission. If you're wealthy, there are exorbitantly expensive facilities, and for the poor and homeless treatment is available free of charge. Family programs can usually be found as adjuncts to every variety and venue.

Examination of a cross section of treatment facilities would reveal that overall not one is more effective than the others. The lamentable high relapse rate appears across the board, and the explanation most frequently offered is that the denial of the patient was insurmountable. Since overcoming denial appears most frequently to be the principal objective of treatment, and since they have been at it so long, one would expect that they are by now quite good at breaking denial. They are. It isn't failure to break denial that explains relapse, it is failure to address the issues of recovery that exist *beyond denial*. Hence, the title of this book.

In the chapters that follow we have addressed a deeper, more characterological level of denial that persists despite the valiant assaults upon it during treatment. We refer to it as the oppositional personality, and suggest it might even be considered a specific personality disorder in its own right. Again, even our view of denial is beyond what persons commonly understand the word to mean.

We wish to make clear that this is not a book on how to stop drinking. It is not an intervention text designed to persuade troubled addicts to enter treatment. It is not intended as a replacement for existing treatment programs. Generally speaking, existing treatments do a bang up job, and a job that needs doing.

The object of what follows is to identify the issues that lie *beyond denial* and to suggest some ways of addressing them. Many persons come out of traditional treatment, and far too many of them and their family members are destined for heartbreaking relapse. We urge them to go this extra mile. There are others who elected to abstain from   alcohol before addiction progressed to so drastic a level that inpatient treatment was indicated. This book is designed to meet their needs as well.

Also it is not a book that deals just with alcoholism. In the interest of brevity we have used the terms alcoholic and alcoholism to represent all addicts and addictions. We have also used the masculine pronoun to indicate both male and female.

I wish to honor the memory of the late Ray Hughes, brother in Christ, counselor extraordinaire, and founder of Community Christian Counseling in Hollywood, Florida. Heaven's gain is most surely our loss. Hail and farewell, old friend.

Patrick Caffrey

CHAPTER ONE

It's the Gospel

Do You Want to Get Well?

I'm telling you, *it's the gospel truth.* Why begin a look at addiction with the word gospel? Well, first of all, gospel is often used to indicate something that is irrefutably and absolutely true. Secondly, the word comes to us from Old English where it meant *good news.* Those who struggle with addiction – the addicts as well as those long-suffering loved ones whose lives are touched by theirs – can surely use some good news as well as assurance that the news is true.

The good news is that the addict is the one who gets to decide. If you suffer from addiction, your answer to the question – *Do you want to get well?* – will determine whether you recover. And that's the gospel truth.

So we begin by jumping feet first into an old, familiar Bible story. We're running the risk that some readers will close the book right now with a sigh, a groan, and a "here we go again." *Just another preacher wanting to get in his licks.* We urge you to stick around. You may be surprised. Incidentally, I'm no preacher.

What we're about to do will set the tone for the whole book which we really hope you'll hang in there and read all the way through. We're going to take a new look at something so old and familiar that many of us have stopped looking at it at all. Here's the way that old story was told 2000 years ago by a fellow called John.

Now there is in Jerusalem near the Sheep Gate a pool, which in Aramaic is called Bethesda and which is surrounded by five covered colonnades. Here a great number of disabled people used to lie – the blind, the lame, the paralyzed. One who was there had been an invalid for thirty-eight years. When Jesus saw him lying there and learned that he had been in this condition for a long time, he asked him, "Do you want to get well?"

"Sir," the invalid replied, "I have no one to help me into the pool when the water is stirred. While I am trying to get in, someone else goes down ahead of me."

Then Jesus said to him, "Get up! Pick up your mat and walk." At once the man was cured; he picked up his mat and walked. (John 5:2-9 NIV)

There we have it, short and sweet. "He picked up his mat and walked." There's that familiar line proclaiming the miraculous healing of the cripple at Bethesda. For many readers that's the end of the story, and we may have become so certain of the outcome, that we don't pay much attention to the way in which the story developed. True, it's about a miracle healing in an encounter with Jesus. But what do we know about the person who was healed, and what do we know about how and where the healing took place? We could say we don't know the answers to those questions because the writer doesn't tell us, or because the details don't matter. What's important is that a miracle took place. Actually there's a lot more information given than we realize. Let's look again.

Now there is in Jerusalem near the Sheep Gate a pool, which in Aramaic is called Bethesda and which is surrounded by five covered colonnades.

The story is set in the Roman province of Judea in the time of Christ. The specific locale is a public gathering place where there is a pool of sorts, and it is surrounded by roofed porches where people can gather to rest and pass the time shielded from the elements of sun or rain. The area is called Bethesda which means *house of grace.* We are also told it is located near the Sheep Gate, which was one of the principal entrances to the walled city of Jerusalem. The Sheep Gate got its' name because sacrificial animals, many of which were sheep were brought into the city through this portal on the way to be sacrificed. Appropriately, it was situated within easy walking distance of the temple. There would have been a lot of traffic consisting of worshippers on their way to make sacrifices, especially on high holidays, and many passers by would have been exposed to the sight of people gathered by the pool of Bethesda.

We can guess that this part of town was not the most attractive neighborhood despite the fact that it was near the temple. The coming and going of travelers as well as livestock on its' w ay to be slaughtered; the braying and bleating of animals and the shouts of their herders with their eyes on a buck to be made; and the sound and smell of blood-letting, dying and burning coming from the temple – these didn't lend themselves to high end real estate listings. Then, add to all of this the following note:

Here a great number of disabled people used to lie – the blind, the lame, the paralyzed.

Definitely no Central Park, West.

Legend had it that the waters of Bethesda, fed by an underground spring, had miraculous, healing powers, and for this reason so many disabled persons gathered there. However, there were conditions which restricted the extent of the healing. Periodically the waters would be stirred as by a tremor in the earth, and it was believed that an angel passing by was the cause. It was also believed that when the water was stirred, the first person (only the first) into the water would be healed of his affliction. All others would have to wait until the next stirring of the water.

Obviously such a system favored the less afflicted who could outrun the more severely handicapped in what must have been a frantic dash to the water's edge each time the shout went up from the crowd that the water had moved! Conceivably, some unfortunates might spend days, even weeks waiting unless they had friends or family to assist them.

One also wonders what sustained these people while they waited. The more afflicted, the longer they waited, and the more afflicted, the less capable they would have been of working to support themselves. For the more disabled, is it possible that the process of waiting day after day and relying on the charity of others to feed and care for them may have led to an attitude and lifestyle of indolence? Is it possible that for some of these persons, waiting at the pool of Bethesda was the first century equivalent of living on Skid Row? Let's return to John's story.

One who was there had been an invalid for thirty-eight years.

At this point we meet the one who is about to get his miracle. John doesn't tell us his name, but in order to relate to him on a personal, present day level, we'll call him Charlie. Charlie, the cripple. Charlie, we're told has been in pretty bad shape for quite a long time. Specifically, Charlie had been unable to walk for 38 years.

Let's do the math at this point. We're told in Luke 2:41 that Jesus' parents went to Jerusalem every year at the feast of the Passover. Assuming they took Jesus with them, once a year he had occasion to see the people gathered at Bethesda. We can imagine the curiosity that spectacle stirred in the mind of a growing boy. We know for sure Jesus was in Jerusalem when he was twelve years old. Luke tells us about that occasion when he recounts the incident of finding Jesus discoursing with the learned doctors in the temple. In John's story, Jesus is an adult about 33 years old. Charlie has been crippled longer than Jesus has lived. How many times had Jesus seen him among the blind, the lame, and the paralyzed? Perhaps the sight of Charlie, still there after all those years is what drew Jesus and led him to single Charlie out and ask:

Do you want to get well?

Typically we don't consider the tone of Jesus' voice or the expression on his face when he asked this question. But given the circumstances, isn't it possible that Jesus may have emphasized the word, *want*? Imagine this:

"For heaven's sake, man, you've been lying around here most of your life and all of mine. Surely there's some effort you could put into getting some help besides lying around waiting for a miracle cure. Tell me honestly. Do you *want* to get well?"

Put this way the question is whether Charlie is at Bethesda seeking healing or is he there to take advantage of the misguided compassion of persons whose pity and self-consciousness prompt them to give him hand-outs? Charlie's response is quite revealing. Just as anyone who has been doing anything for 38 years, Charlie is an expert, and the ease with which he side-steps the question speaks volumes.

"Sir," the invalid replied, "I have no one to help me into the pool when the water is stirred. While I am trying to get in, someone else goes down ahead of me."

Charlie has not answered the question. Instead, he has made a statement to justify his doing nothing to help himself and to elicit pity that hopefully will end with a 'contribution.' At this point in the narrative, t he similarity between Charlie and an alcoholic begins to surface. Typically, the alcoholic has a rehearsed litany of excuses and alibis he recites each time he is asked to do something that will help in his recovery.

As noted, Charlie is an expert at this behavior. It's almost as though he sees what's coming next. The fact that he has refined his line to the level of spontaneity suggests that it has been effective in the past. The expected result is the hand-out requiring no effort on his part, or at least a compassionate offer to remain with him until the next stirring of the waters when Jesus would carry him to the pool. That would fit the traditional characterization of the gentle savior filled with compassion for those who suffer. Significantly, Charlie did not ask for that assistance and probably hadn't been asking for it for the past 38 years. Had he been asking for help on a regular basis, it's reasonable to guess that at least one person would have come to his aid. Once again, Charlie, do you want to get well? Come on. Answer the question.

Pause to consider how the story might have gone had Charlie's answer been a simple *no, I don't want to get well?* But, what possible reason could anyone have for not wanting to walk? A moment's thought may remind us that persons who can walk have more responsibilities than those who cannot. Simply put, if Charlie could walk, he'd be expected to get a job.

Would Jesus have overridden Charlie's expressed preference to remain crippled? Would he have grabbed him by the scruff of his neck and dragged him to his feet, forcing him to walk? Not very likely, for the relationship between God and man is contingent upon man's freedom to choose, including the freedom to resist the will of God. This is free will. And so we have the image of Jesus sadly walking away, honoring Charlie's free will.

But Jesus doesn't bother to ask again, and at this point he forsakes any sappy sentimentalism and gives Charlie what must have seemed like a harsh and even cruel directive to those standing by. Imagine the indignant by-stander intervening to say to Jesus, "What's wrong with you? Can't you see the man is a cripple?" Especially after Jesus said:

"Get up!"

Once again the question arises as to what if Charlie had done this or that? His most natural response after 38 years should have been, *I can't.* Again we have the image of Jesus' sad departure, and the loss of a miracle. But this, for whatever reason, was to be Charlie's lucky day. For whatever reason, on this day, Charlie chose obedience. He did what he was told, and John tells us:

At once the man was cured; he picked up his mat and walked.

Charlie took some responsibility for his own recovery. Charlie obeyed. Charlie did what he was told.

Now is the story over? Will Charlie live happily ever after, going about the city walking and leaping and praising God? Or could it be that he, like 90 percent of the alcoholics whose stories parallel his, will eventually relapse, and return to the life of the cripple? If Charlie does relapse, the danger is not so much that he will begin walking with a limp, but that he will return to the lifestyle devoid of commitment, responsibility, productivity, and fulfillment that resulted from his affliction. Getting well means more than being able to walk just as it means more than not drinking for the alcoholic.

True healing lies in living the abundant life we've been promised.

Will Charlie relapse? John doesn't say. But as we follow the narrative to its' conclusion, we can see a few red flags on the road ahead.

(1) Charlie has a 38 year history of waiting for miracles instead of seeking help in solving problems.
(2) Charlie is something of a whiner and prone to self-pity.
(3) Charlie has a touch of the manipulator in the way he tries to get others to feel sorry for him.
(4) Charlie probably doesn't have much of a work ethic which may be why Jesus put him immediately to work carrying that mat.
(5) Charlie doesn't have any insight into his own recovery.

The last of these items may be seen as we follow Charlie after he leaves Bethesda and ventures forth in the direction of the temple. He is carrying his mat which was probably a kind of wooden pallet wrapped with rags. As Charlie approached the temple he was confronted for violating the law.

The day on which this took place was a Sabbath, and so the Jews said to the man who had been healed, "It is the Sabbath; the law forbids you to carry your mat." But he replied "The man who made me well said to me, 'Pick up your mat and walk.' "

This is a reply from someone who passes the buck, a dangerous practice for anyone wishing to walk in prosperity. Obedience is one thing – essential to Charlie's recovery – but blaming one's decision to obey on someone else has the old, familiar ring of "*I was only following orders.*" Moreover, Charlie is dangerously close to fingering Jesus for inciting others to violate the Sabbath. And if we parallel Charlie's story with that of an addict seeking sobriety, not only do we see blaming others for one's actions, we see compliance; which is doing the right thing for the wrong reason. Blaming and compliance are forerunners of relapse.

Here's a side note regarding the question as to whether John's story might be a metaphor for salvation, and not just about healing. This doesn't seem very likely, for we are told:

> So they said to him, "Who is this fellow who told you to pick it up and walk?" The man who was healed had no idea who it was.

It appears that Charlie did not know Jesus. Moving on, Charlie encounters Jesus again, this time in the temple where he's given the world's shortest and simplest aftercare plan.

"Stop sinning or something worse may happen to you".

The jury is still out on the matter of Charlie's relapse, but Jesus' final statement implies that he's not out of the woods by any means. Charlie has been given a clear warning that unless he makes some serious lifestyle changes, the consequences will be worse than not being able to walk. Suffice it to say that beyond his encounter at Bethesda, there is much work to be done to secure his wellness.

It's also important to remember that some miracles result from the working of a power greater than ourselves combined with our own obedient cooperation. It's wise to keep in mind that a mountain-top experience requires some effort on our part. It's up to us to climb the mountain.

Here's one, final, interesting observation before we close. The miracle that Charlie had been waiting for didn't come in the way he expected. Charlie never got in the water. In fact, his healing had nothing to do with the pool at all.

CHAPTER TWO

Addiction

What's Wrong with You?

Don't you just hate that question? Especially when the one asking it is your own reflection looking hopelessly back at you from the bathroom mirror? We've all heard it. Every one of us makes mistakes, and when we do, there's always someone, like the friends of Job, ready to say there's something terribly wrong with us.

Aren't the results of mistakes bad enough without the added burden of thinking something's wrong with you? Somewhere in our minds we connect *wrong* with immorality and punishment. Punishment means more bad stuff's on its' way, and there's a good chance the bad stuff will include rejection because we've been found unacceptable. And suddenly the image in the mirror is looking at us with loathing. Wait a minute. That's *my* reflection in the mirror, and that look is self-hatred.

We're going to be talking about addiction. Hopefully we're going to discover how to deal with it. But how in the world can anyone be expected to open himself to the possibility that he may have an addiction if he's facing condemnation? The question is rhetorical; the answer is obvious. One reason the alcoholic denies he's alcoholic is that he has enough problems already.

The first thing we'll have to do is agree to stop using the word *wrong*. The power of that word to send us reeling is not what's needed here. Instead, let's agree to acknowledge that certain things we think, say, or do don't get the desired results. Another way of putting that is to say certain things just don't work. At the risk of diminishing the richness of Scripture, for the time being let's say it's a collection of do's and don't's. The do's will work. The don't's won't.

While we're on the subject of the word of God, the apostle Paul indicates that Christians are the *righteousness of God.* That doesn't line up with the idea of someone who is unacceptable and loathsome – someone to be cast into everlasting fire. But how can we explain these righteous ones making such whopper sized blunders? Simple. We act according to what we believe. Some beliefs are true. Some are lies. The true beliefs lead to choices that work. The lies lead to choices that don't. And here's the key to a great deal of problem behavior: our beliefs are learned, and sometimes what we've learned isn't true. What if the teacher came to work drunk everyday?

We're going to turn our attention to the specifics of addiction in just a moment but first we wish to emphasize that there is very little difference in the kinds of difficulties the two groups face – the groups being addicts and those we'll call normal. The two roads diverge when it comes to the way each responds to problems, but the problems are basically the same. We'll look at this difference in greater detail as we continue.

In the text that follows, in the interest of brevity, *alcoholic* and *alcoholism* are used to indicate all addicts and addictions since the principles being dealt with apply to all. Also, the masculine pronoun is used even though an equal number of women suffer from the various addictions including substance and behavioral dependencies.

We will also set down the following definition as a point of reference: *addiction is a learned response to pain in which the individual seeks to eliminate pain without addressing its' cause.*

There are two kinds of addiction: *substance* and *behavioral.* The former involves things we ingest – like drugs. They change brain chemistry. This brings about a change in our emotional state as we go from pain to pleasure, and the *good feeling* is why we go back for more. Alcohol and narcotics are sources of substance addiction. Drugs and alcohol are what usually come to mind when someone mentions addiction.

A behavioral addiction is focused on repetition of certain actions that produce a result like substance addiction.

27

Gambling and work are possible sources of behavioral addiction. A gambling addict continues rolling the dice until he loses everything. The workaholic will work and neglect other aspects of his life (including his health) until he loses everything or until he collapses.

In either case what the addict does seems pointless to the outside observer. Even though it always creates problems in the addict's life as well as the lives of others his life touches, it doesn't strike the addict as pointless. The addict sees what he does as purposeful and effective. He imagines himself in control of the outcomes of his conduct, and it seems that he doesn't learn from his mistakes. It seems impossible to persuade him to change. The elusive purpose behind the addict's drinking or gambling is at the heart of his refusal to quit. Putting it simply, the alcoholic drinks to change the way he feels and unless he is a stark, raving, crazy person with fried brains, the change he desires is to go from unpleasant to pleasant feelings.

By the way, in most cases the feelings are emotional, not physical. However, sometimes people find painkillers to be the gateway to addiction. Even then, people using medication for physical pain may also be attracted to the high they get from the meds. Here we see the double purpose, which is to relieve pain and attain pleasure.

It's a well understood principle that the successful attainment of one's objectives is a powerful reinforcer of the actions one takes to achieve his objectives. This is a fancy way of saying we usually remember what works and do it again. With this in mind, we would guess that addiction must work. It does work inasmuch as it changes feelings and this explains why the alcoholic doesn't want to stop. Over time, he learns that his addictive behavior *does* change the way he feels, and over time, he relies more and more on the addiction. Over time, he fails to learn other ways of achieving his goals.

Eventually, the addict finds himself with no alternative coping mechanisms, just an endless line of new problems the addiction creates. There are lost friendships, unemployment, a broken marriage, failing health and loss of self respect. The addict must face them all with only one solution for every problem. Then he finds himself compelled to repeat that solution which continues to cause additional problems until his own life overwhelms him.

To be sure we stay on track, let's remind ourselves of our definition: *addiction is a learned response to pain in which the individual seeks to eliminate pain without addressing its' cause.* He does this by means of some mood or mind altering substance or a behavior that stimulates a change in perception and mood.

An alcoholic with a toothache drinks to numb the pain instead of going to a dentist to deal with the cavity behind his toothache. He acts as though the toothache is the problem. He also acts as though there is no such thing as a dentist. He overlooks the fact that the pain is only a warning there is a problem – the cavity – which, left unattended will worsen. When the effects of the alcohol wear off, the toothache will have worsened and even more alcohol will be needed. The bottom line of our story is, the cause of pain will grow until the amount of alcohol needed to kill the pain will be enough to kill the addict as well.

This is a dark picture, indeed, and a cause for despair if treatment were not available. However, for treatment to work, it's necessary that the addict admit and accept that he cannot save himself, and that he does not know what to do. This requires a submission to the appropriate authority. In short, he must do what he is told, something he usually doesn't want to do.

The toothache story is more than an isolated example. It's a metaphor for the course of every addiction from alcoholism to codependency. Yes, codependency is a behavioral addiction. That's a matter for another discussion. Let's just say for now, that sometimes people become addicted to each other. We'll summarize by saying that all addiction shares the following characteristics:

1. Addiction is either substance or behavior centered.

2. Addiction is learned.

3. Addiction is a response to pain.

4.   Addiction is pleasure seeking.

5.   Addiction ignores the true cause of pain.

6.   Addiction causes problems.

7.   Addiction is treatable.

Traditional addiction treatment works toward overcoming denial. This is true of Alcoholics Anonymous where the subject is invited to state, "I am an alcoholic," and to *admit* that he is powerless over alcohol. It's also the goal of increasingly intense treatment approaches that include aggressive group therapy like that in residential, rehabilitation programs. All are directed at getting the subject to see the evidence of his alcoholism; to commit to abstinence; and to submit to the authority of those who can help him avoid relapse. When the subject is considered out of denial, formal treatment ends, and he is directed to maintain his 'sobriety' by attending Twelve Step Groups such as AA.

This is all to the point and appropriate. Any flaw rests in the fact that the alcoholic may fail to pursue the path of personal growth toward 'spiritual awakening' that is outlined in the twelve steps. Alcoholics Anonymous should be more than just reinforcement of the first two or three steps. Unfortunately, too often it is not.

Contrary to popular belief, addiction is not defined by the substance. That is, alcohol alone does not produce alcoholism. Nor does the presence of persons we depend upon produce codependency. Addiction isn't defined by the amount of substance consumed or its' strength; and it is not determined by the frequency with which the individual uses the substance or engages in the behavior.

Other popular misconceptions concerning addiction include the belief that addicts cannot abstain. This idea that an addict is someone who *can't live without it* is perhaps the most common fallacy regarding addicts. Alcoholics are imagined to be out of control sub-humans wandering from place to place craving a fix or obsessed with that next drink. The image becomes one of persons who are antisocial – unable to meet their responsibilities regarding jobs, home and family, or to comply with the law. They are identified as skid row bums who can't stop drinking. However, many alcoholics have been known to abstain indefinitely, if need be.

And so, when these false criteria are missing, denial is reinforced and those in denial insist they do not have a problem. True, they may not exhibit the obvious symptoms noted above, but the conclusion that they are not addicts is based on false premises, and the absence of certain conditions is beside the point.

This doesn't mean these conditions don't appear when addiction is present. Substance dependence is a progressive condition and the severity of symptoms increases over time. Because of progression, the untreated alcoholic will eventually exhibit all the aforementioned symptoms unless he dies first. The rate at which the progression takes place can't be predicted. One doesn't have the luxury of saying he has plenty of time, and that he'll get around to dealing with the problem soon. A common expression born of that line of thinking became the title of a book on intervention -- *I'll Quit Tomorrow*. Meanwhile we're reminded of the movie title, *I'll Cry Tomorrow*.

It should also be noted that untreated addiction continues to progress until complete loss of control does occur. In advanced stages of addiction, most, if not all of the easily recognized symptoms will appear. However, failure to recognize this progressive condition until bad comes to worst remains the most tragic aspect of substance dependence.

Accurate Definition

Let's go back to what defines dependence. Earlier we identified two groups; addicts and normal people. What distinguishes the addict from the normal person? In the answer to this question we find what essentially defines addiction.

The difference between the addict and the normal person lies in the way each has learned to respond to his own pain. This statement contains two critical concepts: the concept of *pain* and the concept of *learned behavior*. We won't get into the argument about whether addicts are born that way – heredity versus environment. There is ample evidence for both positions. We'll acknowledge that addiction is produced by a combination of factors, but we're going with the idea the alcoholic's ways are acquired as he grows.

Abstinence

We'll need to address the question of abstinence. Simply put, alcohol isn't the cause of alcoholism, it is the catalyst and drinking alcohol is one of the learned behaviors in the addictive pattern. The alcoholic learns to drink in response to his pain and stress, and therefore drinking is a practice that must be discontinued. Moreover, recovery from addiction is a learning process utilizing one's mental capacities. Alcohol is a mind altering drug which interferes with the brain's ability to process information accurately. It impedes learning. Lastly, the learning of what amounts to an entirely new lifestyle is an arduous undertaking calling for a lot of motivation for change. Persons in recovery who reserve alcohol consumption as a viable alternative behavior in the face of stress will invariably discover their motivation for the process is lost.

The bottom line is that one hundred percent abstinence from alcohol and all mind and mood altering substances not prescribed by a physician who is fully cognizant of the individual's condition is absolutely necessary to recovery. The addict who is not willing or able to commit to this requirement is not ready for recovery. To attempt treatment without abstinence results only in wasting time, energy, and money. It also breaks the hearts of loved ones who have been longing and praying that the addict will be restored to them.

We must also address the belief that abstinence alone will solve the problem. It will not – any more than parking a car will fix a flat tire. On the other hand, one can't change the tire while traveling at 90 miles per hour. How often the alcoholic has been told by well meaning loved ones that his problem is drinking and that if he stops drinking, everything will be fine. It won't, and the alcoholic knows it won't. He has probably already tried 'not drinking' and discovered that everything was not fine.

This also raises the question of what should be done first. When alcoholism is present, it is *primary*; that is, regardless of how many issues there may be, the alcoholism must be addressed *first*. One doesn't put a new roof on a burning house.

Why Do Alcoholics Drink?

The active alcoholic cannot or will not answer this question honestly. For him, beer, wine, and whiskey are not beverages, although he may insist on calling them that. They are conveniently designed devices which deliver the drug, ethyl alcohol, across the blood-brain barrier where it interacts with neurotransmitters and produces changes in the alcoholic's emotional state. Once this happens, the addict's goal has been met. He feels okay. After that, it's all down hill through intoxication to withdrawal.

There are other effects of alcohol, such as impaired social judgment and the loss of muscle control, but the alcoholic does not drink to become obnoxious or to fall down a flight of stairs. Alcoholics drink to change the way they feel. All attempts to attribute alcoholic drinking to other causes are wasteful methods of denying or avoiding the problem.

It bears saying again. ***The alcoholic drinks to change the way he feels***. He does this because he is driven by unpleasant, painful emotions; (most often anxiety) and not being psychotic, he wants to be free of his pain. Sadly, he has not learned effective ways to cope with his pain. He may have learned how to deal with many tasks, and he may seem a high functioning member of society but he lives with hidden pain. When the pain escalates, drinking is the only choice left to him. This is what happens when he relapses. Notice all the references to pain? Addiction sure isn't about having fun.

Since relapse prevention is the first goal of treatment after denial's broken, the addict will need to revisit the sources of his pain. He needs to remember things he has been trying to forget. The difficulty of this step is underscored by the fact that the alcoholic has lost touch with his own feelings. Several terms to identify what has happened come to mind:

denial, suppression, repression to name a few. The process usually takes place before any encounter with alcohol. It happens in childhood when emotional stressors are strong and there is little opportunity to learn coping skills.

What the alcoholic has learned is to *not feel*. Pretending the pain is not there is more effective than one thinks, and over time the mind manages to lose conscious contact with it. Through a number of tricks that include dishonesty, manipulation, and avoidance, the individual detaches from his own emotions. When a person succeeds in losing touch with his feelings, he becomes clinically depressed. By the way, the belief that depression means sadness is not entirely accurate. Depression is best described as the absence of feeling.

These 'tricks" help explain the question that began this discussion. "What's wrong with you? Why do you tell lies? (Dishonesty) Why do you take advantage of people? (Manipulation) Why are you so irresponsible? (Avoidance) Why do you always get drunk? (Last resort) The answer is simple. He's trying to outrun his pain.

Emotions

The use of the word *'feeling'* in place of emotions is unfortunate. It suggests that one must *feel* the emotion for it to exist. The alcoholic concludes that if he doesn't feel it, it's not there. He insists he isn't angry, afraid, or sad, but all this means (assuming the patient isn't drunk) is that his denial system is working well. He's out of touch with his feelings, which is why he's prone to whatever behavior the hidden emotion drives him to, often without his knowing why. (Angry people hurt people; fearful people avoid things and other people; and sad people grieve deeply, seeking solace in the wrong places.)

When he's out of touch with his feelings, he's vulnerable to relapse. And so the immediate goal is to reconnect the alcoholic with his feelings. This will help him see his feelings are part of who he is; that they serve a purpose; and they can work for him. He must learn to embrace those feelings and then learn appropriate behavioral responses. Learning to recognize and identify his feelings is the next step in recovery.

Tacked up on group therapy room walls of treatment centers across the nation are "feeling wheel" charts. They are, as the name suggests, large wheels divided into compartments along the radius, each of which contains a word which identifies a feeling. The purpose of the wheel is to help the alcoholic 'name' his feeling. There may be as many as 50 of these labels, and the only certain result of staring at the wheel for any length of time is to become confused and anxious, and perhaps annoyed, and to withdraw further. There are too many feelings to choose from.

The more simply issues can be identified for the recovering alcoholic, the more likely he is to get to the core of his problem. So we have reduced the feeling wheel to a simple circle divided first into upper and lower semicircles labeled respectively *pleasant* and *painful*, and with each semicircle divided into thirds labeled *peace, love, joy, fear, anger,* and *grief.* A drawing of this wheel can be found on page 40.

There are only six basic emotions. Many of the terms in the expanded feeling wheel are synonyms or indicate varying degrees of intensity of the basic six. When a patient says "I'm not *angry*; I'm *annoyed*," the simplified wheel helps him see that being annoyed *is* anger, and that he has been denying the existence of his issue by telling himself that it isn't there. In some cases the old labels are not feelings at all. For example, one might say *I'm feeling confused.* Confusion's about thinking, not feeling. The real issue is what the person

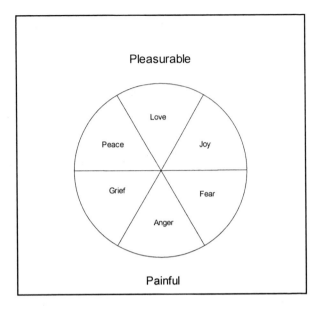

feels when he's confused. For many, it's fear, and if he picks up a drink it won't be to make sense of the confusion. It will be to chase away the fear. And a lot of energy gets wasted trying to resolve the confusion instead of helping the patient learn how to address his fear.

Let's remind ourselves that the addict must be about the business of reconnecting with his feelings which are likely to lead to relapse, so he can begin learning new coping methods. He'll need to own his feelings. He'll need to be able to say "this fear is my fear and I am responsible for deciding how I will react to it. "Without taking ownership, the feeling owns the person, and the feeling determines the person's reaction. In most cases, the reaction is to drink.

The addict in recovery can make use of the feeling wheel as he keeps a daily log of significant events that trigger specific feelings. The log should include the following information: date/time of occurrence; a brief identification of the event; and the feeling. A sample log is shown below. A feeling log can focus attention. It helps emphasize that the person does have feelings. It will also help to identify those feelings that recur and which may be clues to the presence of issues that need to be addressed to avoid relapse.

Date/Time	Event	Feeling
10/15 6:00 AM	Lost car keys	Anger
10/15 12 Noon	AA Meeting	Peace
10/15 2:00 PM	Meeting with boss	Fear
10/15 11:00 PM	Insomnia	Anger/Fear
10/16 9:00 AM	Little League	Anger
10/16 6:00 PM	Jill canceled date	Anger

In the sample log there are six entries in a two day period. Four of the six events triggered anger. The addict, working with a counselor or therapist will likely conclude he has an issue with anger. Before treatment the addict would have seen the anger as the problem, unless he chose to blame it on the events and cast himself as a victim. This is because a definitive characteristic of addiction is to focus on the pain instead of its cause. An addict with a toothache drinks to kill the pain. A normal person goes to a dentist.

Remember the toothache. Treating the pain instead of the cavity will not solve the problem. When the painkiller wears off, the cavity will have grown, and the pain will be worse. This unreasonable approach comes from not learning problem solving skills. This desperate reliance on painkillers is typical of all addicts. It also applies to the approach the active addict will take with emotional pain -- in this case, with anger.

But this is a new day, and our alcoholic should be about learning something new, for he has resolved not to drink, and he is definitely angry. He is at a crossroads, and he will either relapse or find a better way to deal with his pain. He will either do something that doesn't work, or he'll find something that does. I f he chooses the former, he'll do it alone. If he takes the sober route, he'll get some help.

As we close this discussion we'd like to recall our earlier observation that we all act according to what we believe, and that sometimes our beliefs are false. The beliefs that should concern us are not those that merely exist in our heads and which are easily changed when we're presented with new information. An example of this sort of belief might be an incorrect phone number or address.

A different kind of belief is the one that we hold in our hearts. These are not easily changed because we acquired them developmentally over time, and they've been woven into the fabric of our lives and are now an integral part of our personalities. Heart beliefs are part of who we are, and difficult to change. When such a belief is untrue, it can wreak havoc with our lives. For example, if someone says in his heart, *I believe the measure of my worth is in my performance,* not only does this belief run counter to Christian teaching, it will lead to choices that don't work. It is this sort of false belief that is the cause of so much pain. False beliefs are the genesis of countless fears: fear of failure, fear of rejection, fear of punishment, and fear of being found out – and being shamed.

False beliefs are the underlying causes of our confused thinking, our painful emotions, and our ungodly actions. Sorting all of that out is the work of recovery. That's certainly a lot more than just quitting drinking.

But for now, if you suspect you're the one we've been talking about, please remember: the question isn't "what's wrong with you?" The fact is, you're quite special, and there're some words in Scripture you might want to think about: *Behold I set before you this day life and death, blessing and cursing. Choose life.*

CHAPTER THREE

Denial

The Oppositional Personality

Whenever we find ourselves faced with a situation we wish weren't true – let us say news of some tragic event or a serious illness -- often the first thing we say is, "oh, no." No one likes bad news and that short phrase sums it up. We don't want it to be true. Dear friends are getting divorced or a loved one is dying and so, at least for the moment, we deny the news. For the moment we are in denial.

This first response to bad news is so common that we call it *normal.* Under normal circumstances, when bad news is irreversible, we must pass through a series of stages that get us to the point where we accept the thing we cannot change. This process from denial to acceptance we call grieving. It is a series of emotional responses to the loss of something very valuable to us.

As we approach the subject of denial, for many of us this may be familiar ground and some of us may be thinking, *here we go again.* Here comes another diatribe on the subject of denial. However, rarely do addictions therapists treat denial as a phase of the grieving process. We will do well to remember that the addict who commits to abstinence is losing something he values highly and that his denial is more than recalcitrance. He is being asked to say good-by to his best friend – alcohol. His denial is one step in a process that he must work through. It is not wise to insist that he get out of denial as if he were being ordered to stop chewing gum.

Grief is a healing process. It restores us to physical, mental, and spiritual stability after the shock of a heartbreaking experience. Grief should not be hidden, because its' outward signs tell those who love us that we are struggling and in pain and in need of their support. Hiding our tears isolates us in time of need. The Gospel of John reminds us that even *Jesus wept* and it's interesting that after this unabashed, public display of grief He turned His attention to performing one of His most astounding miracles – raising Lazarus from the dead.

Let's compare this to the way someone else (we'll call him the oppositional personality) reacts to bad news. He might say something like:

Leave me alone.
I know what I'm doing.
I can handle it.

This is the hue and cry of one who has heard some disturbingly bad news which he desperately wishes were not true. It is the voice of a man in the first stage of grief. It is the cry of an alcoholic in denial.

It should be noted that the aforementioned healing process is not always effective, and when it's not, it's because the person gets stuck in one of the stages. Most often it's the denial stage. Although precise statistics on the number and frequency of alcoholic relapses are not available, largely due to a tradition of anonymity among recovering alcoholics, a probable estimate would be that 90 percent of alcoholics relapse within a year of the time they decide to quit drinking. Given the severity of the problem of addiction and the extent of the problems it causes, this is a frightening statistic. If a pediatrician or an obstetrician lost nine out of ten patients, he'd be run out of town.

But this sort of thing has been happening to alcoholics for thousands of years. The underlying cause is that most alcoholics, including those committed to recovery, are stuck in denial and we say categorically that an alcoholic who remains in denial is going to relapse. It's just a matter of time.

If this is true, then surely treatment should be directed at overcoming denial. And it is. Every assault upon alcoholism from Alcoholics Anonymous to long term, residential treatment devotes the major portion of its' efforts to eradicating denial. And still they relapse. This is not because treatment approaches are incapable of dealing with denial. Rather, the problem is the result of an incomplete view of denial. The term is most often applied to persons who insist they don't have a problem with alcohol, and insist there's no need to stop drinking. This is one level of denial –

the one which the first step of Alcoholics Anonymous addresses by stating, "We admitted we were powerless over alcohol." No recovery will take place until this occurs, but we can't consider treatment completely successful just because it does.

A person is not out of denial simply because he admits he's alcoholic. That's only the beginning. Note the phrase, "you are in denial." The denial we said always leads to relapse is not something we do; it's a state of being, and a way of thinking. It's a way of responding to life's stressors characterized by *failure to acknowledge or respond to facts.* Sometimes it is deliberate. Sometimes it is unconscious. Always it avoids the truth. It's usually the first and often the last line of defense against whatever one finds to be unpleasant or painful. This denial has all the marks of a personality disorder and it doesn't disappear because the alcoholic admits he has a drinking problem.

We're going to turn our attention to certain critical questions: (1) how does the alcoholic get stuck in such a state of denial; (2) what factors prevent him from getting unstuck; and (3) can we discover a way to help him get this tar-baby to turn him loose?

It will help if we remember the things we said characterize the alcoholic's denial. When he says, (1) *leave me alone,* he's flying in the face of Genesis 2:18. *God said, it is not good that the man should be alone.* When he states, (2) *I know what I'm doing,* he sets the stage to reject wise and loving counsel. When he insists, (3) *I can handle it,* he cuts himself off from desperately needed help.

Let's begin by asking how the addict became such a breeding ground for denial in the first place. The origins of denial are found in the place we find the beginnings of addiction itself. It is the place the future alcoholic spends his developmental years, for this is where he learns what to expect from the world as well as the methods he'll use to cope with it.

Generally, the addict spends his childhood in a dysfunctional family setting. Often he is exposed from the start to the turmoil of life with an active alcoholic. We should emphasize that it's the family dysfunction, not the alcoholism that is the source of the problem. There can be dysfunction without alcoholism, but alcoholism sets the tone for and models the behavior of the oppositional personality who will one day be stuck in denial. In other words, alcoholism doesn't produce denial; dysfunction does. But alcoholism sure can grease the skids.

If you're sensing this discussion is headed for the argument that we are products of our environment, you're right it is. A great deal of what we are does appear to be learned. However, before proceeding further down that path, let's acknowledge some newly discovered genetic factors in the origins of addiction that have come to light through neuroscientific research.

Recent research confirms that there is a particular gene which codes for lower than normal density of dopamine receptivity in the brain and which may be involved in addiction. The link to addiction would be that decreased dopamine receptivity may leave the person more sensitive to stressors and increase the likelihood of his becoming dependent on outside sources such as drugs or alcohol to compensate for what is lacking within.

Also, and perhaps even more interesting, is the possibility that the same gene may code for an inability to learn from negative experiences. The research is incomplete at this point, but it may be that persons genetically prone to addiction may also be unable to learn from their mistakes. This would account for the apparent insanity of alcoholics who insist upon repeating behaviors in the face of evidence that what they're about to do doesn't work. What therapist, working with a struggling alcoholic, doesn't know the exasperation of watching his charge step right back into a situation in which he has recently relapsed?

This issue never speaks so loudly, nor do recovering alcoholics shout so loudly as in the matter of male-female, romantic relationships. Addicts are told over and over not to initiate new relationships with the opposite sex during the first year of recovery because it invariably leads to relapse. Persons in early recovery are not stable enough to cope with the pressures. Over and over the alcoholic returns to such situations and insists he can handle it. (We've used the phrase *handle it* often enough that it might help to call attention to the similarity between the words *handle* and *manipulate*.)

Denial? What seems to be a refusal to face facts and which is often called insanity, may simply be a matter of things not having been learned. Perhaps it's more of a learning disability than all out stubbornness. Should research bear this theory out, the case for a new approach to alcoholic recalcitrance is *huge!*

Returning to the learning paradigm, the common denominator in all addiction is anxiety. We might more simply call it fear, but fear implies awareness of the thing feared, and the addict's early experiences teach him to repress the details of his fears. The ability to pull this off – to repress feelings -- is the essence of denial. But eventually the repressed fear finds a crack in the armor, and it surfaces as anxiety – a vague sense of discomfort accompanied by the thought that something bad is going to happen. It's even more frightening because he doesn't know what it is. The anxiety may intensify and become a panic attack whose symptoms mimic a heart attack. Now he's afraid he's dying, and the need for something to quiet his fear is critical. Somewhere along in here he may discover alcohol. Somewhere along in here it may become impossible to get him to stop drinking.

What is the true source of his anxiety? It's in the family of origin. In worst case scenarios there is outright violence in the home. This can include physical, sexual, verbal and emotional abuse, often at the hands of an active addict. Even without the violence, there is dishonesty, distrust, disrespect for others and for oneself. One lives with inconsistency, unpredictability and irresponsibility. The young child learns to deny problems instead of solving them. Communication is poor at best and often nonexistent. There are broken promises, failed commitments and unfaithfulness.

An air of angry antagonism teaches the individual to be oppositional, often taking an argumentative position that he hasn't thought through. Because he has learned he has no value outside of what he can produce and that his performance determines his worth, he has a need to be right. He may find himself taking a position that flies in the face of facts, because he must not fail. He must not be wrong and when, despite his insistence that he only wishes to discuss things, it's clear he's getting angry, rest assured he's stuck in denial. Unless he resorts to shouting others down, he will probably lose the argument. Either way, he feels sadly alone.

He lives without affirmation, and cautiously picks his way through a domestic minefield in which any moment someone's temper may explode. When it happens, he is often blamed. He learns to be guarded. That unsettling anxiety comes over him whenever he finds himself in unfamiliar places. Put simply, the child who lives in a dysfunctional system learns that the world is a dangerous, unsafe place in which to live. This is the source of his fear.

Over time, these conditions are more than the individual can bear, so he becomes more and more skilled at pretending. His denial is reinforced by other family members who agree to pretend that problems don't exist. This brings to mind the metaphor of the family that lives with an elephant in the living room. Everyone accommodates the elephant but no one ever talks about it.

Now we come to three unwritten, unspoken rules of conduct. Each family member is aware of the rules, having incorporated them into his lifestyle without having been told to do so. The rules are as follows:

(1) Don't talk. (2) Don't trust. (3) Don't feel.

A more careful examination of these rules will reveal that they lend themselves to denial. *Don't talk* doesn't mean one must never speak. Someone has to say "pass the ketchup." The rule refers to not talking about or confronting serious problems present in the home. Primary among those problems is the alcoholism – the elephant in the room. The lesson learned is obvious. This family doesn't solve problems. This family denies the existence of problems, which means a family member will oppose any outsider who even mentions the elephant in the room.

Now those outsiders give rise to the second rule. *Don't trust* anyone who threatens the status quo. This attitude leads to messages that identify strangers as dangerous. Statements like "it's nobody's business what happens in this house" result in fewer and fewer friendships and more and more isolation for the young person trying to find his way into adulthood. The individual also learns to distrust anyone within the family as well. Distrust from the broken promises and the overall dishonesty that pervades the household makes for a painfully lonely life.

Rule number three is the inevitable response to pain when to talk or to trust is forbidden. *Don't feel* means learn to deny your pain.

Pause for a moment to reflect on the way you feel when you break a rule and you will get some inkling as to why these rules are obeyed. When we break a rule, whether by accident or by intention, our belief that wrongdoing leads to punishment makes us anticipate some negative consequence. When we think something bad will happen to us, we feel anxious. Run a red light; get a ticket. Break a rule; get anxiety. For someone who has learned to live by the *don't talk-don't trust-don't feel* rule, isolation is the way to avoid anxiety. "Leave me alone," he snaps. This isn't arrogance. It's fear.

When a person believes his value depends on his productivity and that his performance determines his worth; and he has also learned he must not trust others, two very sad and fearful realities raise their heads to confront him. First, he must do everything well or be discarded like something flawed; and second, he is completely on his own with no one to talk to; no one he can trust; no one to turn to for help.

"I know what I'm doing," he shouts. This isn't self assurance. It's denial. And he's afraid.

It helps to be mindful of the concept of repression. Repression is the function of the unconscious a person uses to stop *feeling his* emotions. The use of the word feeling to mean emotion is unfortunate because it suggests an awareness of the emotion. However, we can lose touch with emotions. This is what happens when someone obeys the *don't feel* rule. When this happens, the alcoholic may deny that he is anxious or fearful.

Sometimes the way to help the individual identify his feelings is to focus attention on thought patterns or behaviors that are present even though the feeling is hidden. For example, the alcoholic may change the subject or avoid certain people, places, or things when he is repressing anxiety. He may inappropriately make jokes to hide discomfort. Or, as previously noted, angry people do angry things; fearful people avoid things and other people; and grieving people may turn to the wrong kind of person for solace. Often the behavior betrays the feeling that has found a hiding place in the unconscious.

Let's summarize by identifying those factors which contribute to the recovering alcoholics remaining in denial and which will lead to relapse if they are not addressed. They are:

(1.)   Alcoholics' brains are genetically coded for dopamine receptor deficiency.

(2.)   Their brains may be genetically coded so they fail to learn from their mistakes.

(3.)   Alcoholics in denial have social anxiety.

(4.)   Alcoholics in denial experience anxiety when confronted with problems.

(5.)   Alcoholics in denial experience anxiety when asked to trust others.

(6.)   Alcoholics in denial tend to be spontaneously oppositional to the ideas of others.

(7.)   Alcoholics in denial are angry.

(8.)   Alcoholics in denial try to manipulate their feelings by manipulating others.

(9)   Alcoholics in denial repress their emotions.

These nine factors provide the material for a treatment plan that will address denial that leads to relapse.

Because the common denominator with all alcoholics is anxiety, finding the sources of the anxiety will help the therapist and patient decide together how to build a treatment plan. Treatment modalities may vary. In some cases medication under the supervision of a psychiatrist may be appropriate. Desensitization may be called for in others. Whatever specific details your treatment includes, the essential requirement is the building of a working relationship with others who will give you wise and loving counsel. You must decide to trust someone.

Emerging from denial, we pass through five stages:

Denial -- Refusal to acknowledge the problem. There's no concern for relapse at this point because the addict refuses to abstain.

Compliance – Doing the right thing for the wrong reason. Often the alcoholic comes under such pressure from family members, employers, or the justice system that he agrees to get help just to avoid the consequences of not doing so. We call this the "get back" stage. The addict's motive is to get back his family, get back his job, or get back his freedom. Relapse is just around the corner, waiting for his ulterior motives to evaporate. When his wife doesn't come back, he drinks. And sometimes when his wife *does* come back, he drinks.

Admission – Acknowledging the problem. This represents an improvement over compliance, but the addict continues to quarrel with reality. He seems angry with the world, a time bomb ticking off the days toward relapse. Eventually, exhausted by his anger, he drinks.

Acceptance—Being at peace with the problem. The addict has come to terms with his addiction. He is no longer at war with reality and he sees his condition as an opportunity for personal growth. There is less likelihood of relapse at this point but it may occur if the alcoholic clings to the belief that he knows how to get well. He starts to design his own treatment plan. Because he's sure he can handle it, he drinks.

<u>Surrender</u> – Submitting to authority of those who can help. Ultimately this final stage is a spiritual one. Because he sincerely believes that he is powerless to save himself and with a newfound faith and confidence in God's love for him, the alcoholic makes a decision to obediently place himself in God's care. The clear evidence of having reached this stage is his willingness to do as he is told.

Now, what's the disturbing, bad news you need so desperately to deny? The news is that you are alcoholic and you know what that means. You will have to give up drinking if you're to be healed. It's disturbing because your drinking has become more important to you than anything or anyone else. The evidence is there even though you don't see it. Ask the ones who love you – your spouse, your parents. Look into the children's eyes. They know. Deep within your heart of hearts you know you are dependent on it. You treasure it. And *where your treasure is, there will your heart be also.*

But all this will stop being important when the barriers of denial are removed and the road to acceptance is clear.

And remember always: there is someone who earnestly desires your recovery and who has the power to bring it about. That one is God.

May you find Him now.

CHAPTER FOUR

Relapse Prevention

Quitting Was the Easy Part

Well, you finally did it. You've been telling them all along, you could. "Anytime I want," you said. "I can do it anytime I want to." And you were right. You went and did it just like that. You quit.

Quit what? Well, that depends on what *they've* been nagging you about and saying you have a problem with. Was it cigarettes, caffeine, drugs, gambling, shopping, the internet, pornography or that old standby, alcohol? Let's say it's alcohol. That's a common habit *they* keep saying people should quit. But just like that, *you* quit drinking. Of course you hate to say "I told you so," but here it is; how many days? And you brought it off without a hitch. You've done it. You can quit anytime you want to.

Now, you must admit you feel pretty good about yourself, and your wife and kids seem pretty pleased with you too. The last few mornings there seemed to be a lot of smiles around the breakfast nook and there was that bit of friendly conversation over coffee. And last night … well you know. Come to think of it, the last few days have really been nice at home, at work and back at home again.

Most of all, it's nice to know that you can quit whenever you want to. Of course you're not going to start back up right away. No point in getting everybody upset. But still, it's good to know you can quit whenever you want to.

Fast forward several weeks. The scene is a holding cell at the local police station. It's 1:00 AM. Our subject has been arrested on a charge of driving under the influence of alcohol and he sits, head in hands, trying to figure out what happened.

There was that sales lunch he had with a couple of old clients. He had been handling their account for so long they were more than business contacts, they were old buddies. The waiter approached and asked if the gentlemen would like something to drink and when it came to him, he said "nothing for me thanks." That launched an astonished barrage about how no one ever knew him to turn down a drink, followed by everyone urging him to order something. Someone used the term, *party pooper*. He ordered ginger ale and had a glimpse of the deal he hoped to make going south.

When the lunch ended he found himself driving back to the office feeling as though he had been hit by a truck. As the adrenaline pumped, resentment rose in him -- resentment toward *them*, the unrelenting *they* who had pressured and nagged and badgered him into quitting drinking. *They* had embarrassed him in front of his friends. *They* had jeopardized his ability to make a decent living. *They* were stealing his joy. That night at dinner, he was quieter than he had been lately.

A few days passed, and he couldn't get the incident out of his head. Driving home from the office, the familiar neon beacon outside his favorite tavern caught his eye and without giving it a thought, he pulled into the parking lot. As he gracefully glided onto the stool and comfortably rested his elbows on the familiar wooden bar top, an equally familiar feeling of peace came over him. When the bartender approached and greeted him like the dear old friend he was, he was thinking, *I can quit anytime I want to.*

Double Scotch neat, he said. Now it is 1:00 AM, and soon *they*, or at least she would be coming to bail him out. He'd see the thinly veiled anger and the hurt disappointment in her eyes. He knew what was coming but he couldn't quite fathom what had happened. Well, our friend is an alcoholic. And he relapsed. When his brain clears, perhaps he'll notice that relapsing was easier than quitting.

Abstinence as a Prerequisite
We must stress here that relapse prevention requires abstinence from all addictive substances or behaviors

including those the addict may never have been exposed to. Many a person has relapsed because he decided to replace alcohol with Xanax. Reference to *substances or behaviors* acknowledges two categories of addiction. In the first, the addiction involves an ingested substance such as alcohol or some other drug. In such cases it is easy to define abstinence and one can readily appreciate the meaning of 100 percent. It's less clear with some behavioral addictions. For example, if a woman has an eating disorder, say bulimia, she isn't addicted to food. Even if she were, one can't abstain from eating. However, in this case the addiction is behavioral That is, the individual depends on certain eating patterns (in this case binging and purging) not upon a substance. Therefore it is the eating pattern that must be eliminated. Other behavioral addictions such as gambling call for 100 percent abstinence. This is true of any behavior that isn't essential to normal, human functioning.

Another important warning that must be heeded concerns the fact that substance dependency is not limited to specific drugs of choice. Substance addiction is addiction and the person addicted to one drug will need to abstain from all drugs with addictive qualities. For example, it is never safe for an alcoholic to use benzodiazepines, or for a crack addict to drink alcohol. This is true even if the addict has never been exposed to the alternate substance. Summing up, the addict must abstain from all mood and mind altering substances unless prescribed by a physician who has been informed of the subject's dependency.

That having been said, we must emphasize that the treatment of an addiction cannot proceed until abstinence is secured. The subject of this message, relapse prevention, refers to what happens beyond abstinence, with the full understanding that a return to active addiction is due to the failure to follow the necessary program of prevention.

Some of *the following information, because of its importance is being restated here as it appears in Chapter Two.*

Why Do Alcoholics Drink?

The active alcoholic cannot or will not answer this question honestly. For him, beer, wine, and whiskey are not beverages, although he may insist on calling them that. They are convenient devices which deliver the drug, ethyl alcohol across the blood-brain barrier where it interacts with neurotransmitters and produces changes in the alcoholic's emotional state. Once this happens, the addict's goal has been met. He feels okay. After that it's all downhill into intoxication and on to the hangover.

There are other effects of alcohol, such as impaired social judgment and loss of muscle control but the alcoholic doesn't drink to become obnoxious or to fall down a flight of stairs. Alcoholics drink to change the way they feel. All attempts to attribute alcoholic drinking to other causes are wasteful methods of denying or avoiding the problem.

It bears saying again. *The alcoholic drinks to change the way he feels.* He does this because he is driven by unpleasant, painful emotions; (most often anxiety) and not being psychotic, he wants to be free of his pain. Sadly, he has not learned effective ways to cope with his pain. He may have learned how to deal with many tasks and he may seem a high functioning member of society but he lives with hidden pain. When the pain escalates, drinking is the only choice left. This is what happens when he relapses.

We might say that when the alcoholic drinks it's because he's experiencing painful emotions which he has no other means to alter. He's also going straight for the feeling with no thought of what's causing it. He's like a man with a toothache who never heard of tooth decay or dentistry. He's doing the only thing he knows how to do.

Since relapse prevention is the first goal of treatment after denial's broken, the addict will need to revisit the sources of his pain. He needs to remember things he has been trying to forget. The difficulty of this step is underscored by the fact that the alcoholic has lost touch with his own feelings.

Several terms to identify what has happened come to mind: *denial, suppression, repression* to name a few. The process usually takes place before any encounter with alcohol. It happens in childhood when emotional stressors are strong and there is little opportunity to learn coping skills.

What the alcoholic has learned is to *not feel*. Pretending the pain is not there is more effective than one thinks and over time the mind manages to lose conscious contact with it. Through a number of tricks that include dishonesty, manipulation, and avoidance, the individual detaches from his own emotions. When a person succeeds in losing touch with his feelings, he becomes clinically depressed. By the way, the belief that depression means sadness is not entirely accurate. Depression is best described as the absence of feeling.

These 'tricks" help explain the question that people often ask. "What's wrong with you? Why do you tell lies? (Dishonesty) Why do you take advantage of people? (Manipulation) Why are you so irresponsible? (Avoidance) Why do you always get drunk? (Last resort) The answer is simple. He's trying to outrun his pain.

Emotions

In Chapter II we took time to explore the work that needs to be done by the recovering addict to regain conscious contact with his repressed feelings. We established that failure to do so will leave him vulnerable to relapse. This is because undetected, painful emotions generate behavior that runs counter to sobriety. Learning appropriate methods of dealing with painful emotions rather than resorting to alcoholic drinking under stress cannot be meaningful unless the emotion is correctly identified.

It's wise that we take a moment to comment on the ease with which the addict can slip into learned, alcoholic behavior which has become second nature to him. The alcoholic's maladaptive behaviors have become so ingrained in him as to be part of his personality. As muscle memory enables us to drive an automobile without conscious thought about what we're doing, so can the individual in early recovery easily revert to old ways, especially under stress.

The addict has already mastered the patterns of conduct that make him alcoholic. Now he is faced with the task of learning a whole new pattern, called sobriety, while at the same time trying to forget the old. He's like someone learning a foreign language while being forbidden to use English. Should he find himself under severe stress – let's say he's fallen from the roof of a tall building -- in which language will he most likely cry out to God? Won't it be the old, familiar, forbidden English?

There is much work to be done to maintain awareness, especially his awareness of his own feelings. It's advisable that the reader review the material on addiction in Chapter II, paying close attention to the diagrams of the feeling wheel and the sample feeling log found on pages 41 and 42. A thorough understanding of the function of these tools and the processes followed in using them is prerequisite to the material that we are about to consider.

Let's Do This Thing

The recovery process must address two things: (1) learning to identify the cause of the pain, and (2) learning how to eliminate the pain by eliminating its' cause. That seems simple enough. Then why did it take so long to get here? You tell me. Perhaps it has something to do with the difficulty in getting the addict to listen. But let's assume everyone's listening now. Let's be about the business of finding the cavity in the tooth.

We're going to look at a sequence that leads to action. In the case of the active addict or the one who relapses, the action would be his picking up a drink. Double Scotch neat. The sequence is as follows:

(1)   Event

(2)   Belief

(3)   Thought

(4) Feeling

(5) Action

Each element proceeds directly from the one that precedes it. However, when some of the elements occur the individual isn't always aware of them. When this is the case, he's only partially in control of what happens. Sometimes he's only aware of the event and the action that follows. The belief, the thought and the feeling, may be hidden somewhere in the recesses of his mind.

For example: police respond to a call about a disturbance at a neighborhood saloon. They discover that one man has bloodied another's nose. When asked to explain, the attacker says, "I hit him because he said Bobby Cox is an idiot." (Bobby Cox is the manager of the Atlanta Braves.) We see only two elements here: an event and an action and to the assailant, the incident makes perfect sense. Still, he can't tell you what underlying belief led to his behavior. Nor does he have an answer to what he was thinking or what he was feeling. *He said it, and I hit him.*

With such limited insight, a person is likely to believe that events cause behavior. This leads to the belief that events must be controlled in order to avoid inappropriate behavior. *I wouldn't have had to hit him if he hadn't said that about Bobby.* This produces control freaks who spend most of their days unhappy and frustrated. The truth is that events don't cause behavior or feelings and even if they did, we can't control everything.

Events don't cause our decisions. Instead, they trigger certain beliefs, and those beliefs are the basis for our decision making. If what we believe turns out to be untrue, the action that follows will be inappropriate. Here's an example of an appropriate action based on a belief that's true.

Most people believe that wild *grizzly bears are dangerous animals.* This belief usually has little bearing on our actions. We don't decide not to go to the super market because bears are dangerous but, finding yourself inside a locked cage with a grizzly bear is an entirely different matter. The *event* triggers your *belief* about bears, and you think "I could get mauled or killed." That *thought* activates the *feeling* of fear which prompts you to *action*. The action will either be to try to escape or to call out for help.

This brings us to an important fact about beliefs that will be important as we continue. What we believe doesn't have to be true to influence our decisions. We just have to believe it. The example of the bear in the cage could easily go the other way if, due to a bizarre set of circumstances, someone believed that bears are like little lambs -- warm, cuddly, harmless creatures. Person's holding this belief will be inclined to change it after a first encounter, that is, if they survive.

When the belief we hold is untrue; that is, a lie, the entire sequence is affected negatively. Consider this. When the belief is untrue, the thoughts it generates are confusing thoughts. Confusion leads to painful feelings, and finally painful feelings motivate ungodly action. By ungodly, we mean action which runs counter to God's plan for the greater good in all of our lives. We haven't introduced such terms as sinful or evil at this point in order to avoid an air of condemnation. We wish to keep the focus on the fact that ungodly behavior doesn't work. For the alcoholic an example of ungodly behavior is his picking up a drink. A graphic of this paradigm is found below.

Unpleasant	**Event**
Untrue	**Belief**
Confused	**Thoughts**
Painful	**Emotion**
Ungodly	**Action**

Although in most cases we acquire our basic beliefs growing up, and although experience adds to those beliefs and reinforces them over time, sometimes in crises an experience can be so painful and powerful that it alters the personality immediately and unforgettably. Such a crisis usually involves the serious wounding of the child followed by the intrusion of heart rending lies.

When a child is deeply hurt by an experience and unprepared to cope with the pain, he must turn to adults for protection and comfort to get him through the emotional turmoil. At this point the child is highly impressionable, and is most likely to receive whatever message he is given as gospel truth. The m essage is spoken (or unspoken) by the parent whose job it is to guard the heart of the child.

A simple example might be the three year old who falls and cuts his knee. When he runs in tears to his mother she gathers him in her arms and as she holds him close, she soothes and assures him that he is all right. He believes her, and in a few moments his tears are gone. At the moment of wounding, his mother possesses the power to heal.

And there is much more to her message than a few words of comfort. In the way she responds to her son's pain, she assures him that he is loved, and that he is valued, and that he is safe. She dropped everything else for him. What a wonderful gift! He will remember moments like that forever. And in a few years when she begins to teach her child about the love of God, it will make perfect sense to her child because the *more perfect love* that casts out fear has been reflected in her loving kindnesses to him.

71

Let's look at another, less fortunate child. She is a seven year old daughter of alcoholic parents. They are completely absorbed in their daily drinking and they neglect her. This little girl spends long periods playing alone, and one day she is sexually molested by a teenage boy who lives next door. There is no one to run to in her confused and wounded state and when she cries herself quietly to sleep that night, wondering why this terrible thing has happened to her, the enemy of her soul whispers into her heart.

This bad thing happened to you because you are a bad little girl. Nobody likes bad girls. God doesn't love you anymore and nobody cares about you. Nobody will ever love you.

The lies are confirmed in the unavailability and the silence of her alcoholic parents and because no one else is there for her, she believes. She won't forget the lies, and one day years from now she'll be telling this story to a therapist. And she'll be saying *I'm afraid no one will ever love me.*

The mind is open to a great number of beliefs and we haven't world enough and time to explore each one of them. We can, however, identify four basic beliefs that seem to be at the root of all confusion, pain and ungodliness. We'll state each one as if we were expressing a personal belief. We recommend you do the same and that you commit them to memory. This will help you relate to them as your own. What's that? Maybe you don't hold these beliefs? Well, even though you're not conscious of it, to some degree the following statements do apply to you.

(1) I believe I must do well and that my performance is the measure of my value. I fear failure.

This statement, however inaccurate, is an attempt to respond to our longing for goodness. It seeks to answer the question, what makes me righteous or *how am I justified* before God and men?

(2) I believe I must be approved of and accepted by others and that others are the judges of my worth. I fear rejection.

Here we come face to face with our need to be connected, as well as our awareness that it is not good to be alone. That awareness is a reflection of our separation from God. The belief is a distorted, shallow means of achieving reconciliation.

(3) I believe that persons who fail or do wrong are unworthy of love and should be punished. I fear condemnation.

The law of the Old Testament states there must be consequences for wrong doing – an eye for an eye. We call this justice, a restoration of balance and a return to the way things were before they were disrupted by wrong-doing. We seem to think that it's our responsibility to restore the balance and so we go about trying to do well and to *bring offenders to justice.* We assume that God is looking on, waiting for us to propitiate Him.

(4) I believe that I am what I have done and failed to do and that I cannot change. I fear others will find me out and I'll be shamed.

This belief has its genesis in coming to the end of ourselves. The full impact of our failures finally gets to us and we find ourselves looking in the mirror and asking the question, "what's wrong with you?" We define ourselves by our mistakes and we give up and hide ourselves in shame.

"No way!" you say. "I recognize the falsehood in each of those statements and I totally disagree." Perhaps; but before digging in too deeply and finding yourself unable to climb out of the trench you find yourself in, look at the way you react to events. If you act as though the statements are true, then you believe in your heart they are true.

Have you ever chosen not to take part in some activity – the company picnic softball game, or an evening of karaoke, perhaps – because you're not very good at it? Have you ever kept quiet about your spiritual convictions because someone might make fun of you? Have you ever given someone the silent treatment after they had hurt your feelings?

Have you ever given up on something and said just that: "I give up; it's hopeless?" Have you given up on quitting drinking?

These beliefs are virtually impossible to change, because of the manner in which they were learned. We learned them developmentally as they were acted out in our lives as children. They were woven into the fabric of our lives and became an integral part of our personalities. We learned them unawares and acquired them very early in life. Children are like wet cement, easy to write on, but the cement hardens and what was written in childhood is difficult to erase. And if the beliefs are lies, a life based upon those lies will be filled with confusion, pain and decisions that take us away from the plans God has for us.

It may seem like we're drifting further and further from our stated objective which was to discover how to identify and eliminate the sources of the pain that drives addiction. What may seem like a diversion is intended to establish a firm basis for the conclusions we're working toward. In keeping with this, we're going to look at why the four beliefs cited above are untrue. The argument is rooted in four conditions secured by the sacrifice of Christ.

(1) In His death upon the cross we were made righteous. Our sinfulness was replaced by the righteousness

of Christ and we were justified. All that was necessary was accomplished and our performance is beside the point. We have nothing to prove. God did it all.

(2) Once separated by sin, we have been reconciled with God through the sacrifice of his son. The sin or imperfection that kept us from entering into the divine presence has been removed and we are fully acceptable to the Father. The approval of others is nice, but not necessary.

(3) The law says "the wages of sin is death," and Jesus said, "I have not come to destroy the law, but to fulfill it." The punishment required by a just God has been exacted. God is satisfied. This is called propitiation. It means that this is the time for forgiveness, not punishment.

(4) And finally, from the throne in Heaven we hear "behold, I make all things new," And on the third day He arose again from the dead. This is regeneration at its finest. Who says we can't be changed? Who says we can't begin again?

Now I guess we're ready to package the relapse prevention thing. Remember, the ultimate goal is to change the belief because the belief is the hidden cause of the painful emotion. Keep in mind as well, that these beliefs don't change easily the way we might change our minds about which movie to see. We're going to need some help.

We can analyze a specific relapse pattern and even predict its appearance by following the five part sequence mentioned earlier. To help keep track, we'll use a series of five boxes, labeled with the words: event, belief, thought, feeling, action. See the drawing below.

Event	Belief	Thought	Feeling	Action
A fellow employee and friend blamed me for losing this month's payroll records.	Wrong-doers are unworthy of love and should be punished.	What she did was totally wrong and she's no friend of mine.	Anger	I didn't speak to her for days and I started a rumor she was cheating on her husband.

In this example where the triggering event is a fellow worker unjustly blaming the subject for a mistake on the job, we have entered the belief about punishment being the appropriate response to wrong-doing. This follows through negative thoughts about the offender to anger and finally to retaliation in the form of gossip and character assassination.

Obviously it takes more time to analyze the sequence than it does to live it. This is because most of the elements are unconscious and they don't use up as much time and energy as spoken words do. In fact, the time it takes to go from the event to the feeling may be only a fraction of a second. This is a good time to point out that the time to work on our issues is not when we're caught up in them. Working through an issue calls for quiet reflection. It should be done after the storm has passed. A better time would be before the storm arrives but learning how to do that is why we're here.

As you examine the chart on page 77, ask yourself, if you were the subject, which of the five items in the sequence you would be able to change. First, it should go without saying we don't control the actions of others, so we can't prevent events or change them once they happen. Secondly, we've pretty much concluded our belief system is untouchable. Third, if you think you control your thoughts, try not thinking about red jellybeans for the next 15 minutes. And finally, when was the last time you were able to stop being afraid just because somebody told you to relax. I'll bet you weren't in a dentist's chair. Bottom line? The only thing we have direct control over are our own actions.

This means we have a choice between the godly thing and what we feel like doing. Our angry subject felt like hurting someone, which he did, putting into action the belief that wrong-doers should not receive love, but punishment. The problem is that this won't work. It won't get rid of the anger which is sure to make going to work everyday stressful, and if the subject happens to be an alcoholic trying to achieve sobriety, that anger will be a major relapse factor. What's a body to do?

Let's try obedience. Let's try getting in line with God's plan. We determine what's the godly action and we do it even if we don't feel like it. In the example we've been looking at, the godly action would be to refrain from any hurtful, punishing action and perhaps determine to do something that would bless the individual. Don't go overboard. A pleasant smile and greeting can be a blessing. Will you still be angry? Yes, but it won't last so long. Will you still think the co-worker did wrong? Of course. What about your belief about punishment? It will linger but if you continue to act in obedience and contrary to what's in your heart, you'll discover that a power greater than yourself has begun to change your heart. In AA they say *fake it 'til you make it.* When the heart changes, we think differently and the anger, the fear, and the grief begin to fade.

Well boys and girls, now's the time to say good-bye to all our company. It's time to sum things up. We hope it's clear that what's needed for relapse prevention is change. People who have known an alcoholic before and after sobriety invariably say, *he's a changed man* that's it in a nutshell. Unchanged, the alcoholic will never stay sober.

Preventing relapse requires a different way of behaving that results from a completely changed belief system. We can use the event-to-action paradigm as a journaling format to stay actively involved in the process of growth, change and relapse prevention.

Dear Journal,

I was asked to give a presentation to the sales staff next week and I know several others more experienced than I will be there watching and listening. Several of them are executives from corporate. I worry about how well I do things, what people think of me and I thought a lot about how many mistakes I might make. The more I thought about it the more frightened I became. I have to admit that the thought of having a drink to relax, crossed my mind. It took awhile to shake that thought. I had all but decided to lie and say I was sick and not come in to work the day of the presentation. Then I remembered what makes me valuable. Then I got to thinking how I might help some other salesmen get a better understanding of the product. I've decided to do the presentation. I'll do my best and let God do the rest.
P.S. It's still kind of scary but I'm going to give it a shot.

It makes you wonder how the presentation went, doesn't it? I think it probably went well.

We began this discussion saying the alcoholic drinks to change the way he feels. Let's not forget he's also trying to find peace, love and joy which are the opposites of fear, anger and grief. We need to remember that it's our belief system, not what happens to us, that causes us to think, to feel and to act the way we do. The underlying source of our pain – the cavity in the tooth – is a belief hidden in our hearts and the belief is untrue. Hopefully this material will light the path leading to a new day and a new way.

CHAPTER FIVE

Codependency

It's Not What They Say it Is

Ask five people what codependency is and chances are you'll have five definitions, each of them different, none of them correct. Codependency is one of the least understood of relationships because people think the term explains itself. They define dependency. They put *Co-* in front of it and off they go. Then unsuspecting souls who cross their paths get labeled codependent.

Now, the reason we're concerned with codependency is that it's a problem. Yet many definitions don't seem to point to a problem at all. For example, if dependency is understood to mean reliance, then codependency would apply to any relationship where people rely on each other for *anything*. That sounds like marriage. Yet we're not about to say that marriage is codependency. On the other hand, marriage is a likely place to look for codependent persons. More of that later.

If you're someone who's been labeled, this may help you decide if the label really fits. To begin with, you'll need to know that codependency is not a healthy condition. It's an addiction. Let me say that again. It's important.

Codependency is an addiction. Let's take a moment to remind ourselves about addiction since it too is often misunderstood.

We noted in a previous chapter there are two kinds of addiction: substance and behavioral. The former involves things which are ingested – like drugs. They change brain chemistry. This brings about a change in our emotional state as we go from pain to pleasure and the *good feeling* is why we go back for more. Alcohol and narcotics are sources of substance addiction.

A behavioral addiction involves repetition of certain actions that produces a result like substance addiction. Gambling and work are possible sources of behavioral addiction. Just as a gambling addict continues rolling the dice until he loses everything, the workaholic will work and neglect other aspects of his life until he loses everything.

Summarizing any addiction as *a learned response to pain in which the individual seeks to eliminate pain without addressing its cause,* and noting that he does this by means of some mood or mind altering substance or a behavior that stimulates a change in perception and mood, let's look at codependency with a view to its being a form of addiction. We begin by recalling the aspects of addiction we identified previously. We'll then re-examine each of them as it is reflected in the behaviors of persons who are codependent.

1. Addiction is either substance or behavior centered.

2. Addiction is learned.

3. Addiction is a response to pain.

4. Addition is pleasure seeking.

5. Addiction ignores the true cause of pain.

6. Addiction causes problems.

7. Addiction is treatable.

Number One: Codependency is a behavioral addiction. Codependency relies on conduct and always requires interaction with another person. Also, the more intimate the relationship, the more codependency is likely to flourish. This is why we said marriages are likely places to find the problem. The behavior patterns associated with codependency may be extensive and varied. But the action the codependent person turns to for relief of his pain and attainment of pleasure is behavior devoted to "helping" someone who appears incapable of helping himself. That's why a codependent relationship calls for one person who is weak and another who appears to be strong and can claim the dominant position. On the surface the pattern may seem quite positive. Who would discourage anyone from helping another? However, the motive behind the *caretaking* is not the wish to serve others but to generate a sense of self-centered well-being in the codependent *caretaker*. In short, as the alcoholic *drinks*, the codependent *helps*. Also, as we observe the alcoholic in action, we see he is driven by the desire to maintain control over the alcohol. The codependent also works toward control -- control over the person he helps. This even goes to the point of interfering with the other person's right to run his own life. It is this control, coupled with his belief that he is doing good that gives the codependent a sense of heightened self-esteem.

Number Two: Addiction is learned. Things that are learned include skills, understandings, attitudes and patterns of behavior that we are not born with. We acquire them from our environment. The word, 'learner', may conjure up the image of children sitting obediently at their school desks while a teacher, pointer in hand, instructs them. But our most significant learning we get through immersion. The things we learn from being a part of what's happening around us will so shape us that they become part of the fabric of our personality. They are not easily forgotten, which is to say, they're very difficult to change.

Think about this contrast. Every school child studies English for 13 years in a formal, classroom setting. But, at the age of five, before even stepping inside a school, he is fluent in English. The 13 years only refine and reinforce what was learned at home. This reminds us how a great deal of learning takes place at an early age. It will have major effects on the rest of our lives and we probably won't forget it. Like the spoken language, most of what we learn to expect from the world and most of what we learn about coping with it is learned in childhood. To determine how the codependent addict came to be the way he is, we look to his growing up.

More often than not, the codependent grows up in a dysfunctional family system. In worst case scenarios there is volatility and outright violence. This can include physical, sexual, verbal and emotional abuse, usually at the hands of an active addict. Even without the violence, the system fosters dishonesty, distrust, disrespect for others and for oneself. One lives with inconsistency, unpredictability and irresponsibility. The young child learns to avoid problems instead of solving them. Communication is poor at best and often nonexistent. There are broken promises, failed commitments and unfaithfulness.

The developing child is taught he has no value outside of what he can produce. He lives without affirmation and cautiously picks his way through a domestic minefield in which any moment someone's temper may explode. When it happens, he is often blamed. He learns to be guarded. An unsettling anxiety comes over him whenever he enters unfamiliar territory. Put simply, the child who lives in a dysfunctional system learns that the world is a dangerous, unsafe place in which to live.

Dangerous, unsafe places give rise to fear. When fear is prolonged for days, and then years, it becomes a component of life a nd we call it anxiety. Anxiety, however, isn't the product of danger alone. Danger is the catalyst but the active ingredient is the absence of control. When real or imagined danger presents itself and the anxious one struggles to gain control, he does it to reduce anxiety. There, in a nutshell, is the connection between codependency, anxiety and control.

We wonder why he doesn't try to change his environment, or at least to get out of it. But sadly, this young person needs his environment. Even an infant knows that it's dangerous to be alone. He has no other place to go. Without exposure to other lifestyles, he assumes dysfunction is normal. The idea of changing the system doesn't even cross his mind because it's beyond his experience.

Two choices are left to him. He can follow the example of parents and siblings and be absorbed into the system, or he can learn to protect himself from the system by manipulating it. If the family centers around alcoholism, then to be absorbed means he learns to be an alcoholic. On the other hand, if he goes for the second option, he will learn codependency.

Even if a person doesn't travel the road to alcoholism or some other substance addiction, he will still take on many of the character flaws to which he is exposed. This is so true that sometimes the only way to tell the difference between an active alcoholic and a codependent is to smell his breath.

The growing codependent may try to find self-worth by avoiding the overt alcoholism of his family. (Many codependents swear they will never drink.) Instead, he may establish himself as the one who fixes things. Paradoxically he never feels so good about himself as when there is a domestic crisis that calls for his help. When things are going well, this knight in shining armor becomes depressed and a feeling of insignificance creeps over him. As his codependency grows he begins to seek new crises. He may even create a crisis or two of his own. When he comes of age and it's time to leave home, the knight errant sets off on a quest for a poor, dysfunctional damsel in distress. She may be an alcoholic just like Mom or Dad. Our knight will marry this helpless creature. He believes they'll live happily ever after as she turns to him for every good thing and he provides it. They seem to be made for each other.

We shouldn't leave this topic without saying that most codependent behavior doesn't come from conscious planning. The image of deliberate choices helps us paint more vivid pictures of how codependents act but they have little awareness of what they are doing. If you, the reader, have begun to recognize yourself in the content of this message, you are not being accused of malice to any degree. Most maladaptive behavior is learned unconsciously and remains with us only because it seems to work for us. On the other hand, if you can hear us saying, *"this is what you're doing, and this is why it isn't working,"* therein lies the hope of healing.

<u>*Numbers Three and Four:*</u> Addiction is a response to pain. Addiction is pleasure seeking. We said addiction springs from the basic impulse of every living creature to move away from what is painful while hoping to find pleasure at the same time. Where there is intense pain, the need to escape it is preeminent and the dysfunctional family is a virtual reservoir of pain. The developing codependent applies the avoidance behavior modeled in his family to his need to escape the unpleasantness. Since he can't escape by leaving the family and since he doesn't have problem solving skills, his only option is to view the pain as the problem. His goal is to get rid of the pain with no concern for its cause. He avoids the true problem and manipulates the people instead.

This manipulation has two parts. (1) The codependent accommodates the wishes of others so they won't turn on him. (2) Then he sets about repairing the damage they cause so they'll praise and admire him. The idea is to be liked by everyone. He avoids the pain of rejection and has the pleasure of being needed. This child is often called the *family hero* because his role calls for him to be good at doing so many things. He is the peacemaker, the fixer and sometimes the provider. He is the one the family members point to with pride. He dignifies the entire household.

If this portrait of success seems somewhat empty, it's because the person at the center of it is empty. His life is taken up with manipulating others so he can survive in a dangerous place. There is no vision – no talk of hopes, dreams, or aspirations for the future. There is no joy, no peace, no love. There is only survival.

Number Five: Addiction ignores the true problem. With all the talk about painful circumstances, one may think they're what the codependent should be dealing with. Dysfunctional families do exist and they are troublesome. They require the efforts of anthropology, psychology and theology combined. But, the family unit is the *source* of the problem, not the problem itself. Changing the family won't heal the codependent.

If our codependent were to present for counseling and psychotherapy and the clinician were to suggest he begin working on fixing his family, he'd play right into the hands of codependency. Once again, the codependent patient would find himself trying to manipulate the conduct of others instead of dealing with his own issue. The issue is that he can't change the way he feels or maintain a healthy, happy lifestyle. His issues also include generalized anxiety stemming from his fear of intimacy and the inability to sustain a lasting, meaningful relationship with another human being. That's why, when the therapists asks *"what brings you to counseling?"* he often hears: *My marriage is on the rocks."*

That statement is a distraction to lead us down another rabbit trail to nowhere. It sounds like marriage counseling is in order, but if the diagnosis is codependency, all the marriage counseling under heaven won't help, because the core issue is fear of intimacy hidden behind the mask of Mr. Fixit or Mrs. Helpinghand. The core issue is codependency.

Number Six: Addiction causes problems. Any troublesome action can be found seated between two sets of problems. We'll label them primary and secondary. The primary problems are those that motivate the action and the secondary are those problems the action causes. The toothache story is a good illustration. The toothache is the primary problem that motivates the alcoholic to drink a pint of whiskey. Drinking whiskey leads to the secondary problem of the alcoholic's arrest for drunken driving. We can also add here, another problem which is *dental carres*. That means he'll wake up in a jail cell with a whopper of a toothache.

Up until now most of our attention has been directed at primary problems of codependency. The dysfunctional family is what initiates codependent behavior. Most of us would like to dismiss the secondary problems, but they don't just go away and ignoring them is just another avoidance. In order to prepare for the task of healing that lies ahead, the codependent person will have to identify and take responsibility for the problems his behavior has caused. Here are just a few character traits that may manifest themselves in the codependent. One can imagine what problems they may lead to.

1. Codependents aren't sure what's normal.
2. They start projects they can't seem to finish.
3. They lie when it's just as easy to tell the truth.
4. They judge themselves very severely.
5. It's hard for them to have fun.
6. They take themselves too seriously.
7. Intimacy is uncomfortable for them.
8. They tend to over-react.
9. They worry about what others think.
10. They usually think they're different.
11. They have to be super responsible.
12. Their loyalty is often undeserved.
13. They tend to act on impulse.

The basic problem faced by the codependent is the one we spoke of earlier. It's the inability to enter into and sustain an intimate relationship with another person. Anxiety prompted by intimacy makes the codependent avoid honest sharing of himself with another. Closeness produces an awareness of vulnerability he cannot tolerate. Long ago he learned it was unsafe to share his thoughts or to trust anyone with his feelings. He may have even lost touch with those feelings, and when invited to share them, he is embarrassed and awkward. This lowers his self-confidence.

The need for avoidance leads to behaviors which drive others away. He picks fights, finds fault, or ridicules. Arrogance, hostility, anger, or any number of hurtful things are directed at persons who draw too near. When the target of such behavior is the codependent's spouse, we have the makings of disaster.

A note about intimacy: sometimes intimacy is used to mean sexual intercourse. This may lead to the idea that codependents have problems with sex. This may be the case with some and when it is, aberrant sexual pursuits may surface. These may include pornography, prostitution or going to strip clubs. These activities depersonalize and objectify relationships and do away with the call to intimacy. On the other hand, some may also choose sex as a substitute for true closeness so that sexual intercourse even with a spouse becomes a means of avoiding intimacy instead of fulfilling it. Again the codependent controls persons in his life by manipulating them.

The most definitive, dysfunctional behavior is reflected in the sort of person the codependent is attracted to and with whom he is likely to strike up a relationship. This extends to the dynamic between the participants. Earlier we referred to the participants as the *knight in shining armor* and the *damsel in distress*. The one to whom he is attracted is invariably a weaker personality with low self-esteem and lacking assertiveness. Often this person is an alcoholic. These conditions allow the codependent to retain control over the way the relationship plays out.

Below is a graphic comprised of two horizontal, parallel lines. The upper line is labeled *wellness* and the lower line is labeled *death*. Between the lines is a third line which rises and falls as it moves from left to right. This line is like the path of a roller-coaster, climbing almost high enough to touch the *wellness* line, then falling until it nearly touches the line labeled *death.* The middle line continues this course, up and down, across the drawing surface. It never moves above the *wellness* line or below the *death* line.

Wellness

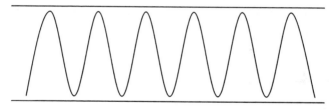

Death

The graphic represents life in a codependent relationship. The participants (one codependent and the other alcoholic) travel together between the lines. If either of them crosses the upper *wellness* line alone, that person becomes well; but the relationship ends, because the other remains behind -- alive and unwell. If either crosses the lower *death* line, this ends the relationship for obvious reasons. There is another possibility. If both cross the upper line, the relationship still ends because the codependency upon which it was founded no longer exists.

So long as the relationship remains a codependent one, neither the alcoholic nor the codependent escapes the relationship. The dynamic depends on the alcoholic relinquishing responsibility for his or her actions and the codependent deriving significance from helping; that is, from controlling another. The trap (and yes, it is a trap) is maintained by the codependent with the consent of the unsuspecting alcoholic.

The codependent often encounters the alcoholic when she is on the downward slope, moving toward the *death* line. He rescues her and sets her on the path toward *wellness.* This may include taking her to detox, getting her into treatment, encouraging her to go to AA and generally supporting her recovery. During this stage of the relationship there is a feeling of love and affection between them.

The relationship follows an upward path until the alcoholic comes dangerously close to crossing into *wellness,* and suddenly the codependent's tactics change. He begins to neglect her and then to attack her personally: her character, her appearance, or her intelligence. He makes deriding comments or resorts to name-calling and public humiliation. As her self-confidence declines, he may take her to dinner and suggest she have just one glass of wine to relax, or he might buy a six-pack and leave it in the refrigerator for her to find. When she relapses under the pressure, he lets her plummet until she's comfortably close to the *death* line. Then he rushes to the rescue and the roller-coaster sweeps upward once more.

Why does the codependent act this way? By now it should be obvious. There is a release from anxiety and a sense of personal well-being in the control he derives from helping someone else. Remember, *helping* is to the codependent what *drinking* is to the alcoholic. The codependent's significance and value depend upon a relationship with someone who is not well. Should the alcoholic find sobriety, the codependent will find himself out of a job. The same applies if the person dies. Therefore both must be prevented. Remember also, the codependent doesn't know how to relate to a well person. Neither can he conceive of himself as being well.

We're approaching the end of this discussion, and before concluding, we need to mention a course of action frequently seen among codependents. It's called *enabling*. Taken out of context, this term has a positive ring to it. To enable means to help but help in the hands of the codependent usually boomerangs. Enabling is anything the codependent does to interfere with the natural consequences of another person's inappropriate conduct. When enabling occurs, instead of learning to change his behavior, the addict will be encouraged to continue his problem behavior because it is without consequence. When the codependent bails the drunk driver out of jail, he encourages him to drink and drive again. Enabling is just another device available to the codependent who wishes to discourage another from crossing over the line into *wellness.* The enabler helps the sick person stay sick.

Number Seven: Addiction can be treated. This brings us to the million dollar question. How can the codependent be helped? If we remember that codependency is an addiction characterized by behaviors that fail to address the underlying sources of pain, then the answer is he must follow the same path the alcoholic or gambling addict must travel to find healing.

This begins with a commitment to abstinence. As the alcoholic must begin by abstaining from alcohol, the codependent will have to compile an extensive inventory of codependent behaviors and begin to eliminate those behaviors from his repertoire. He will probably require the help of a therapist to guide him and a circle of support persons who will hold him accountable.

Incidentally, for the past 70 years recovering alcoholics have been turning to Alcoholics Anonymous for needed support. although not as numerous as AA groups, in some areas there are twelve step groups dedicated to codependency. They may be called Codependents Anonymous.

Putting a stop to codependent conduct does not solve the problem any more than stopping drinking cures the alcoholic. However, recovery can't take place if addictive behavior remains. Recovery calls for change and one cannot change and remain the same.

Letting go of old behaviors helps the codependent realize how his actions have been hiding the causes of his pain. His old behavior tricks him into thinking his problems are solved. A sense of control creates an illusion of wellness. But when the codependent is without those behavioral defenses, the underlying, emotional sources of distress are exposed and open to healing and change. A simpler way of saying that is: *when we confront the cause, we can work on the problem.*

The final leg on the journey calls for relapse prevention. This means learning new ways of coping with old issues. The process is often difficult, more often challenging, but finally rewarding. Don't think what we have said is a call to unilateral action and isolation. The healing of codependency doesn't call for separation. It calls for persons working interdependently toward productive, positive goals. The truly healthy partnership involves individuals who contribute equally to the relationship.

SIX

Adult Children of Alcoholics

In Search of What's Normal

The more we examine the subject of addiction the more we discover the problems it gives rise to extend far beyond the suffering individual. Addiction is a family matter, even though a specific family member may not always become an addict himself. The impact the family of origin has upon the development of the individual and the impact the individual has upon his own, extended family can make for a vicious cycle. Once it's in place, alcoholism corrupts the family which in turn is likely to produce more dysfunction and inappropriate patterns in the generations that follow.

At this point we're going to expand our use of the word *alcoholism* and apply the term to the complex of dysfunctional life-styles it produces. We'll separate these into three main groups: (1) addicts, (2) codependents, and (3) adult children of alcoholics. The separation into groups is for *ease of handling* and individuals may find themselves in more than one category. We have looked at addicts and codependents in previous chapters. That brings us to the third group.

In Chapter Five we mentioned that codependent individuals guess at what is *normal*. This isn't so much a diagnostic pointer for codependency as it is the result of coming of age in a dysfunctional family. We wish to make clear that family dysfunction can generate a variety of conditions including codependency or alcoholism, but that neither is inevitable, and there are similarities and differences between them. But both usually produce persons who have difficulty knowing what is normal.

From here on, we'll refer to this group which may or may not develop alcoholism or codependency, but who historically fit the designation Adult Children of Alcoholics, as ACOA. In the interest of avoiding categorization of all such persons as either drunks or enablers, we'll identify them simply as what they are – adults who grew up in a home where one or both parents was an addict. We'll begin by identifying what ACOA's have in common.

First: they are survivors.

Second: they did without.

Third: they figured things out on their own.

Fourth: they keep secrets.

Fifth: they suspect they could be happier, but they're not sure what that means.

Sixth: they guess at what is normal.

ACOA's are survivors: With so much emphasis on negative outcomes from coming of age surrounded by addiction, we might ask whether anyone can survive the experience without falling victim himself to some dysfunction or another. The operative word here is *survive* and, to be sure, there are those who learn to do just that – to survive. Literally, the term means to emerge from an experience *alive*.

Well, that has a hopeful ring to it, doesn't it? Needless to say, in a truly life-threatening situation, that should be the goal. The alternative is certainly less attractive. However, there can be problems when survival is the only goal. For the person whose anxiety driven perspective causes him to see the world as a dangerous place, there is the danger that he won't learn to set goals or to pursue aspirations beyond survival.

Imagine being asked "well, little boy, what do you want to be when you grow up?" Imagine if the only answer were: *I want to be alive.* Imagine no place in your childhood fantasies for answers such as "I want to be a cowboy, a fireman, an astronaut," with no chance of refining those childhood imaginations into grown-up dreams of becoming an engineer who builds towering sky-scrapers, or a Nobel Prize winning novelist, or a scientist who finds the cure for cancer. Imagine the person whose energies have been completely focused on learning to survive.

Without a doubt the ACOA is a survivor and in a life threatening crisis, the skills he's learned as such will come in useful. We'll probably discover such persons are good to have around in a crisis. But so are fire hydrants. And we can't help but wonder how much of a life does a fire plug have? Ruling out the existence of serious pathology or maladaptive behaviors, there is the possibility that the ACOA might merely become a rather boring, hum-drum individual, much like the *misfit* we'll look at later in this chapter.

The survivor lives with an overriding question. *Is this a safe place?* No doubt that was an appropriate concern in the time of the Altimira frescoes, but the average citizen won't be encountering a saber toothed tiger when he returns home to his hearth tonight. And he won't have to fight off hungry intruders from the neighboring cave. But the ACOA has recollections of growing up when he had to negotiate that domestic minefield we spoke of earlier. His question may be slightly modified to read, *is it safe for me just to be myself?* The answer is often *probably not*. Probably not because in the absence of reliable indicators, he has learned the best course of action is to play it safe and assume danger is around every corner, just a heart-pounding step away.

Danger walks hand in hand with fear. And what does the ACOA fear? He fears what by now we should recognize as *the usual*. There's fear of *failure*, that is, of making a mistake. There's fear of *rejection* or not being liked. There's the fear of being judged and the resulting *condemnation*.

Lastly there's the fear of *being found out* which includes the fear that others will discover his fear.

So much fear calls for an extensive defense system. Look around a social gathering. See if you can spot the ACOA. He's the excellent listener about whom you know almost nothing because he never tells you anything about himself, unless it's said in jest. The constant joking is entertaining – in fact, endearing for awhile but doesn't it distract you from looking at the person, himself?

He may be the sports enthusiast who deflects any scrutiny by pointing to the action on the playing field. If he participates (in any group activity) his part will be carefully rehearsed and refined over time, so he is confident of his own level of competence. If the agenda calls for something new, he's quick to defer to others and to support and encourage them.

He's the faithful, loyal friend who gravitates to the same, closed group of acquaintances he has carefully cultivated over time. He seldom reaches out to embrace newcomers.

His attire and demeanor are moderate, often to the point of being nondescript. His speech is seldom loud and never raucous. When the party breaks up and the group has dispersed, it may be difficult to remember exactly what he looks like.

He's extremely cooperative and an excellent worker and follower. He is never antagonistic and the thought of his starting an argument is unthinkable. He always quietly joins the rank and file and at the end of the day, he is able to say with a sigh of relief, *I made it!* He survived.

One final note: if these behaviors appear to change noticeably when the picture includes an opened bottle of beer held comfortably in his hand, chances are you've found your adult child. Note the oxymoron? *Adult child?*

We need to emphasize that the emergence of the do-little, go-hardly-anywhere individual from the alcoholically dominated family of origin is not necessarily a permanent condition. However, it is not uncommon for such persons to manifest the heart belief referred to earlier that says *I believe I am what I am and I cannot change.* As we have indicated, this belief is untrue and the person in recovery needs to discover that even the ordinary person is more than ordinary and capable not only of changing, but of accomplishing extraordinary things. Jesus said, *I am come that they might have life and that they might have it in abundance.* It's not normal just to survive.

ACOA's did without. This statement could refer to the fact that persons who lived in dysfunctional families frequently were reduced to poverty level living due to the irresponsibility of alcoholic parents. However, material hardship isn't always present and when it is, it's more easily overcome than affect deprivation. The latter, emotional unavailability of parents to their children, has a much more devastating impact on personality. Emotional availability is what makes the difference between successful, intimate relationships and those in which we act as strangers.

ACOA's grow up without intimate, emotional connection with parents and siblings. What's more, they learn to do without it and even come to believe that not having it is normal. This process can begin very early in life and often happens because of the belief held by many that newborns and infants are not affected by things they cannot remember. This is the equivalent of thinking that if you don't feed a baby it won't affect his development because later on he won't remember having been hungry. The fact is that the child who is deprived of affection – and that begins when the child's cries are ignored by parents -- w ill pay a serious price in maladjustment later on.

A safe rule of thumb is that it's impossible to spoil a child during his first year of life. During this time the crying child is expressing real needs and every effort should be made to meet those needs. Unmet needs have disastrous effects and toxic parents don't meet needs.

Sometimes the issue is complicated by the parent's angry response to the child in need which causes him to associate his need for affection with painful rejection. Because of this *pairing*, he learns to fear his own felt need of

109

affection as much as he fears rejection. As he spends his formative years in this hostile environment, the fears are reinforced. By the time he reaches adolescence, he is already devising ways of getting along without affection and intimacy.

In that vein we note that the individual may gravitate toward pornography and other inappropriate sexual activities which gratify affective needs without the demands or stressors that go with intimacy. The result is a totally depersonalized, pseudo-relationship. Later in life honest displays of affection, even something as simple as a man and wife holding hands make the ACOA embarrassed and uncomfortable. Seldom will he initiate an ordinary gesture of intimacy with another person (especially someone of the opposite sex) until he has been reassured that he will not be rejected. He's attracted to gregarious females who take the initiative and who assume the leadership role in the relationship, especially in social situations.

The three rules that govern the dysfunctional system: *don't talk; don't trust; and don't feel* are conducive to maintaining distance between family members, especially during the formative years.

"I never heard my parents discussing things unless they were shouting at each other," is frequently heard from the ACOA. "If I walked into the room when they were talking, they always stopped when they saw me."

"My mother and father always seemed to be giving each other a lot of space. They seemed to be checking each other out, jockeying for position. It reminded me of two wrestlers circling each other in the opening minutes of a match."

"My parents never showed affection and they never said *I love you* to me." These are commonly heard statements that come from ACOA's.

This may be an appropriate time to remind ourselves that the problems resulting from addiction extend beyond drinking issues. The behavior tends to persist after abstinence. The impact of alcoholism upon the behavior and the temperament of ACOA's can be visited upon generations that follow, even when the use and abuse of alcohol ceases to be a factor. Some may observe that alcoholism sometimes skips a generation, but learned, alcoholic behavior seldom does. Conduct such as that noted above does not result from drinking. It results from children modeling their parents' behaviors.

ACOA's figured things out on their own: To some extent, the foregoing material should help explain this factor. With so much isolation, what other course does a person have? It shouldn't take many occasions of being left on his own to convince the ACOA that he is indeed on his own. For pretty much the same reasons he avoids intimacy with others, he avoids seeking help. Somewhere along the way he begins saying, *leave me alone. I can handle it.* Do you know someone who won't ask for directions no matter how lost he becomes? Ask him to tell you about his childhood.

Of course, once the individual has figured it out on his own, it becomes important that his solution be right. Otherwise, having made a mistake, he might be obliged to ask for help. There's a vicious cycle here, threatening to begin spinning out of control unless he can overpower (with anger, perhaps) the person who logically points out that he ought to ask for help. He is apt to stay away from people physically, or most assuredly emotionally so he can handle it alone. Superimpose this pattern on someone who is an active alcoholic and you have a sense of the reaction you'll get if you suggest your drunken friend should get some help.

ACOA's keep secrets: To keep something secret is to keep it hidden. This simple observation helps clarify the motivation for keeping secrets. We hide things we believe are wrong in order to avoid punishment; and we hide things we value so that they won't be taken or stolen from us. The ACOA is never sure about right and wrong if his experience has taught him the correctness of his conduct is determined by the mood swings of a physically or emotionally abusive alcoholic parent. This being the case, the ACOA prefers to conceal as much of what he does as possible.

Sadder yet is the need to hide whatever happiness he may stumble upon. He doesn't share his heart's desires with anyone for fear that ridicule and humiliation will steal his joy. His disappointments and his occasional successes – both end up in the same secret place.

If we recall the first two rules that govern the dysfunctional family, namely *don't talk* and *don't trust,* we see another reason why the adult child is prone to secrecy. The ACOA has difficulty knowing when it is appropriate to disclose information about himself and his family, and when he is faced with an occasion calling for self-disclosure, he becomes anxious. Conversation becomes awkward and stilted. He may even resort to telling lies. The lie allows him to rattle on in great detail about himself because only he knows that what he is saying is not valid self-disclosure.

Addiction and the patterns of behavior related to it such as codependency and the ACOA syndrome have dishonesty in common. The foundational problem of addiction is not the substance. It is the behavior. Typically individuals in treatment hear the statement, *you don't have a drinking problem; you have a living problem.* This indicates the need for the person to change his ways. Two things prevent change from occurring. One is his drinking. The other is his dishonesty. A subtle variation of dishonest conduct is secrecy, and it can be just as much a problem for the children of alcoholics as it is for the alcoholic himself. Sound familiar? *Don't talk; don't trust.*

And so long as the ACOA is obedient to the rules; so long as he keeps secrets; there is a sense of safety because he manages to avoid the anxiety that rule breaking arouses. This behavior becomes generalized to many other aspects of life, and the individual finds himself keeping secrets that shouldn't be secrets at all.

An ACOA may be possessed of some truly good news and decide to keep it to himself. He may have received especially bad news and choose not to mention it. The sum total of the ACOA's secrets amounts to all the things that would answer the request, *tell me about yourself.* The usual reply to this request is, *not on your life.*

We've heard the expression, don't go there when persons don't wish to deal with a particular issue. Under normal circumstances, such occasions are limited in number. However, the ACOA's life is so shot through with unresolved issues, particularly those that have slipped below the radar of denial and the cover of what's forbidden that practically every event that occurs is a potential trigger for false beliefs and unwanted feelings. Almost without exception, the most troubling situations for him are those which call for interaction with other people. Since such situations are impossible to avoid, the ACOA must develop means of interacting with and avoiding people at the same time. One way he accomplishes this is by keeping secrets.

Half a century ago John Powell, SJ wrote a little book entitled *Why Am I Afraid to Tell You Who I Am?* The answer was simple: I'm afraid to tell you who I am because you might not like me. And that is all I have. Interestingly the question and its answer speak of fear. Like the man in the title, the adult child deals with his anxiety by keeping himself a secret.

ACOA's suspect they could be happier, but they're not sure what that means. "Is that all there is?" The lyrics of a once popular song recorded by Peggy Lee ask that question and go on to say that if that's all there is, then just keep dancing. The melody and the rhythm of the song are plaintive, and we can tell the dance is not a joyful one. In fact, the song and the scene it depicts are rather sad.

Sometimes relationships are like that plaintive dance. The dancers turn in little circles, seeming to engage one another while moving in a larger circle about the dance floor, only to arrive back at the place the dance began where nothing has changed. *Is that all there is? If that's all there is, my friend, then just keep dancing.* And so the dancers continue their vain attempts to connect by imitating the behaviors they saw modeled in the past. They antagonize one another, creating a bond of exasperation and anger where there ought to be love.

Surely the dancers suspect there's something else, but a life limited to survival has obscured whatever the something else might be. What's more, out of all the hundreds of thousands of dance partners who might know the answer, each of these dancers has chosen one who doesn't have a clue. Look closely. You may discover that each is the adult child of an alcoholic.

How did they find each other? The answer is really quite simple. Each recognized in the other something vaguely familiar. What each recognized was something dysfunctional, but it was the familiarity that drew them. We tend to equate familiar with comfortable and when an ACOA is comfortable it's because his anxiety has faded. The comfort they felt was a sense of relief when each realized the other didn't expect much, especially in the way of intimacy. Yes, the dancers suspect they could be happier, but they aren't sure what that means. And so they just keep dancing.

ACOA's guess at what is normal. For this we'll need to define *normal.* We postponed addressing what follows until now because defining normal is easier after we've looked at what's abnormal. Normal is one of those hard to define words everyone knows what he means when he says it, but no one can tell you what it means. Two other words that fall into this category are *okay* and *appropriate.* For our purposes here, our definition of normal is a composite of all three. Normal is what most people consider appropriate and about which they say *that's okay with me.* Conversely, if most of the general population considers something to be inappropriate and not okay, then it isn't normal.

We hope the preceding paragraph makes sense because we're going to proceed on the assumption that it does. We're going forward on the belief that once it's pointed out, everyone can see that a certain thing is abnormal. This follows the principle set down in the story of *The Emperor's New Clothes* in which everyone saw the truth when the little child said, *he's naked!*

Should the abnormality of something not be immediately evident, it may be because the reader is alcoholic, codependent, or an adult child or some combination of the three. It may be necessary to get away from the people, places and things you're involved with and spend some time in some place besides the Land of Oz. Be careful though. As suggested above, products of dysfunction tend to gravitate toward more dysfunction and to think it's okay. Of course this means accepting someone else as a qualified authority on the subject. It always comes down to that – trusting someone else. And the someone else has to be the right person. At any rate, what follows are just a few things that, believe it or not, are not normal.

(1) **It is not normal to become intoxicated.** No matter how frequently the people around us may do so, getting drunk is not normal. There is something

unusual, and even bizarre about ingesting toxins until they disrupt brain function.

(2) **It is not normal to hurt people.** Abuse shouldn't be difficult to spot. Abuse hurts people unnecessarily. Abuse may be physical, sexual, emotional and even spiritual. Granted, some abuse is more difficult to discern than all out physical cruelty. That's why the critical question is *does it hurt?* It's not okay to hurt people. And by the way, the saying that sticks and stones will break my bones but names will never hurt me? The last part isn't true.

(3) **It is not normal to use people.** This is our way of pointing out that use of people is abuse. It has been said that we are to use things and love people, not love things and use people. Using people overlooks their true value and to devalue human beings isn't normal conduct. It hurts.

(4) **It is not normal to tell lies.** A man is as good as his word. The successful, productive course of a functional life-style depends on individuals honoring their commitments and speaking the truth. Cheating is not normal. Dishonesty is not normal. Borrowing and not repaying is not normal. Adultery is not normal. Divorce is not normal. *But everybody does it.* Our response to that statement is that we don't know that. But we do know the person saying it does it.

(5) **It's not normal to be alone.** Isolating oneself from others is a common defense mechanism among ACOA's. Scripture states that it isn't good for man to be alone. A closed circle of people gathered behind a closed door or a family devoid of friends or hospitality, familiar though it may be, isn't normal.

This list could extend indefinitely. We're stopping here in order to place emphasis upon just a few not normal conditions frequently found in dysfunctional families and which ACOA's tend to accept as normal behavior. These may help those who have been asked, *why can't you be like normal people?*

To summarize: Normal people don't get drunk; hurt people, manipulate people; deceive people; or avoid people. This should help us get started on the path toward recognizing what's normal in ourselves and in others. If these things still strike you as normal, you may have been cut off from the mainstream of humanity longer than you think.

One more element that applies across the board to ACOA's is their complicity in maintaining the dysfunctional, alcoholic family dynamic. Although the effort is not intentional, each member of the poorly functioning family plays a specific role in the preservation of the unit with all it's inappropriate processes. If we think of the alcoholic family as a poorly managed business desperately trying to avoid bankruptcy, then each member may be compared to an employee of the company. Each person has a specific job description.

The company/employee metaphor is important because it speaks to an aspect of society in which people identify or define themselves according to what they do. Ask the average person to tell you about himself and typically he will begin by saying something like, *my name is Harry and I'm a mechanic.* There will often be a difference in the level of self-esteem evident in the person who says *I am a cardiologist* as opposed to the one who says *I am an unemployed dishwasher.*

This illustrates the importance we place upon the jobs we do. When the job is bound up with someone's identity, then having a job to do is tantamount to being somebody. Isn't that what we mean when we say *I want to be somebody*? We mean we wish to have an identity. Think of the implications of not having an identity – to be nobody – a person without significance or value and a person that no one ever acknowledges.

Now, one way of persuading an employee to remain with a poorly operating business – a dysfunctional family – would be to pay him top dollar. This is highly unlikely in a near bankrupt company. In that case, let's convince him that his position in the company is basic to his identity. Let's arrange it so he believes he's somebody because of his job. This can be accomplished easily and inexpensively by making him vice president in charge of latrine maintenance and then making a big fuss about him. He continues to do the same dirty job, but now he *is* somebody.

If the family is a business, there should be a product. Day after day dysfunctional families are cranking out a wide assortment of human misery and retailing it to an unsuspecting world. There's your product – human misery. The family members see to it that the company stays in business with each member having a job to do and each remaining on the job because that's what gives him his identity. Let's take a look at some of the positions to be had in the typical, dysfunctional family these days.

Chief Executive: First there is the CEO who is central to the operation. He is the active alcoholic who pretty much sets standard operational procedures for the entire family. Although his duties are minimal, there is no under-estimating the power he wields. It's safe to say that every decision made in the company is one way or another influenced by his policies. His only, actual responsibility is to become and remain intoxicated as often and for as long as possible. He is critically important to the rest of the family because he is why each of the others has an identity (a job). Everyone else accommodates him. Everyone is afraid of him, because no one wants to lose his job.

Chief Financial Officer and Director of Operations: This position is usually but not exclusively reserved for the spouse of the CEO. The person seeking this position will need to be a codependent of the highest order. This is an extremely important position because the individual is responsible for keeping the CEO alive and for preventing him from becoming sober. Recalling the material in the chapter on codependency, we said that death or wellness will end the relationship. In this analogy, the business would close up shop and everyone would be out in the street if they lose the CEO.

This master enabler has one of the most difficult jobs because she is required to take up the slack left by the indolent CEO as well as directing day to day operations, and overseeing the other employees. Of course, the individual is amply compensated with a glowing sense of self-importance. Neighbors are sometimes heard referring to her as a saint.

Vice President of Public Relations: Not everyone is fooled, however. The day to day dysfunction resulting from an addictive life style is bound to catch the attention of outsiders who may presume to point out to the proprietors of this Mom and Pop operation that their lives are a mess. Such an accusation requires a proper response if the business is going to continue running. This calls for someone who will improve the company's image and that job often falls to the first born son or daughter.

Even though bringing children into a dysfunctional family is hardly advisable, doing so is almost inevitable because a solitary enabler would find the work unbearable. There is just too much to be done and some of that includes justifying the way things are done. That means someone has to excel in such a way that the rest of the family can point with pride and say, *look what we've done!*

This is the task of the PR Person whose job it is to do everything right. He's a Boy Scout of a fellow who gets good grades, edits the school paper, captains the football team, works nights, assumes adult responsibilities long before his childhood should have ended, gets a scholarship to college, graduates with honors, goes on to medical school and wins the Nobel Prize. When the voice of conscience whispers, *you people are sick,* they point to him and say, *can sick people do that?*

The Prodigal: By the time a second child is born into the business, the family member as employee system is well established and one can picture the new kid casting about and wondering who he is; that is, what's his job? Watching his older sibling in action and seeing all the accolades that befall him, the newcomer might decide he wants to be a PR person too. The message he gets, however, is *sorry, that position's been filled.*

Not to worry, for in spite of the excellent work the PR man has been doing to bring dignity to the family, that still, small voice and a lot of not so gullible neighbors keep saying, *there's something about all of you that just isn't right.* So Mom and Pop decide what this business needs is a prodigal son who can be blamed for everything that continually goes wrong. Whereas the first born does everything right, this new worker is expected to do everything wrong.

He's the rotten apple who will be pointed to as the one spoiling the whole barrel. Generally speaking, he is disobedient, lazy, and disruptive. He does poorly in school, drops out, can't get or hold a job, frequently winds up in trouble with the law and shows up one day for dinner with a ring through his eyebrow and a tattoo. He gets into drugs and alcohol at an early age, and for all intents and purposes follows in the footsteps of the addicted parent. And whenever the still small voice speaks disparagingly of the family, they point to the prodigal and say *he's the reason for our troubles.*

And what's his compensation? First of all, he is somebody. He is also the focus of a lot of attention and he lives a life virtually devoid of responsibility. He has job security because he performs a vital function, that of a scapegoat. He is also well provided and cared for by the enabling family members whose skills must be honed on a regular basis.

The Misfit: Should there be another member added to work in the family business, that person may find it difficult to define him or herself. Occasionally someone is hired when there isn't a job for her to do. Eventually it's discovered this person was hired because he or she is related to the boss. As far as the hardworking staff is concerned, the misfit doesn't belong but the boss' decisions have to be honored. *Don't worry, darling, we'll find something for you to do.*

Meanwhile, the misfit must be careful not to interfere with anyone else's job and so she withdraws from active participation in the daily business. She fades into the wallpaper and manages to avoid doing the wrong thing by simply doing nothing. Eventually a job description emerges for the misfit. The other workers come to expect that she will never interfere with company business, which means she will never add to the chaos of daily life. Her job is to provide calm in midst of the storm. No one worries about what the misfit might do. She won't do anything. Her compensation? She has no responsibilities and nobody dislikes her.

The Entertainer: What's this? Based on the trouble finding a job for that last employee, it would have made sense to stop hiring. Well, good hiring practices and sensible family planning aren't always found in dysfunctional systems. Sometimes, usually after some years, another soul enters the picture. He is sometimes referred to as the baby or the baby brother. For a considerable length of time he doesn't have a job at all. By this point the craziness of the company operations is exacting quite an emotional toll on all the workers and at the end of the day they just wish they could kick back, unwind and be entertained. They could all use a good laugh.

Well, what do you know? The baby is about to be put to work. Before he realizes it's happening, he's in the midst of them, doing funny things and saying funny things. Everyone is laughing and everyone is very pleased. No one has to think about the messed up family. At last, the baby has a job. He's the one who entertains everybody and makes them laugh.

Later, someone will come up with the idea of having him put on a funny costume and letting him do his act outside on the sidewalk for people driving by. They'll say *what a fun place that must be* and they'll come inside and buy our product. In this way outsiders, perhaps even an occasional, normal one may be persuaded to swell the ranks. Recently a popular television sitcom was built around the life of a dysfunctional family in which the normal young wife of the baby of the family had been drawn into the madness when she found herself attracted to her husband because he was funny and cute but had little else to recommend him. Ironically, the role of the immature husband was played by a successful, stand-up comedian.

Having looked at the roles of members of dysfunctional families as well as the "perks" that keep each worker on the job, let's consider the downside. It's a mistake to assume that people who remain at their jobs do so because they are delighted with them. During the Great Depression of the 1930's, very few people thought, *I like my job.* Jobs were so scarce and so essential to survival, a man was happy to even have one. For those living in the midst of addiction, survival is often the first concern – certainly not happiness.

Let's look beneath the veneer of each family type and see what's really going on. We already have enough information about active addicts to know that the **Chief Executive** (the alcoholic) is a disturbed, unhappy, loveless, angry, grieving, anxiety driven individual whose principal goal in life is to be drunk.

Beneath an outward show of competence and control, the **Director of Operations** (the enabling spouse) lives with a sense of powerlessness that drives her to excessive responsibility, manipulation and self-blame. This fragile creature seldom smiles except when she puts on the plastic mask of denial. Life is a deadly serious struggle for survival and her repressed feelings run along the lines of anger, fear, guilt and pain.

For the firstborn **Public Relations Person**, life plays out in quiet desperation. Because his value depends upon his performance, he is constantly reminded that he must not fail. He may enjoy the admiration of others who see him as reliable, affable, a high achiever and an all round good fellow, but this comes at the price of his having been robbed of his childhood. Scratch the surface and you'll discover rage, confusion, low self-esteem, and painful loneliness.

The **Prodigal Son** is the most transparent of the family members. With his acting out and his oppositional-defiant conduct, he wears his heart on his sleeve. He is angry, deeply angry and his sullen affect shows it. But he is also lonely with a fear of rejection that prevents him from honest intimacy with others. He hides a painful sensitivity with an outward show of hostility. In exchange for the attention others give him, he pays the price of being disliked by them. He is often the next generation's addict.

The **Misfit** derives her identity from her lack of distinguishing features that might help to define her. We're reminded of Emily Dickenson's lines, *I'm nobody, who are you? Are you nobody too?* Insecurity, loneliness, confusion and fearful anxiety lurk beneath her outward look of detachment. This is Laura from *The Glass Menagerie* who lives in a world of old phonograph records and little glass animals. She lives and will probably die alone.

Last but not least is the **Entertainer** (the baby.) Protected by a wall of attention-getting, clowning, humorous antics and hyperactivity, this super-cute family pet hides his fragile nature. Under it all he's the least mature of the adult children. His status has not required him to grow up and when he finds himself thrust into the strange world of adult responsibilities, he is afraid, confused, insecure and feels very much alone. Much deeper down he is angry about all this, but he is a master when it comes to hiding anger, even from himself.

Not very pretty, is it? Addiction is a family affair. In the next chapter, we'll look at what the family faces when it seeks to find healing and the addict at the center of the action isn't ready to change.

Here's one final note about the order in which the roles described in this chapter are assigned. We have identified the job descriptions according to the order in which they usually occur. This is not fixed in stone. Some families don't have six members. Sometimes more than one role is assumed by one person or individuals may assume different roles at different times. There are also occasions when individuals may exchange roles with the Public Relations Person stepping down to Prodigal and vice versa, or the Misfit emerging into the limelight while another withdraws.

SEVEN

Family Matters

When the Addict Isn't Ready

Now that we've made our way through the preceding chapter, it should be apparent that addiction is anything but a one person problem and the next time an alcoholic says *leave me alone; I'm not hurting anyone but myself*, it shouldn't be too difficult to refute that outrageous travesty of truth, reason and logic. As mentioned before, addiction is a family matter, and the suffering it causes others is almost enough to make the addict's suffering pale by comparison.

Perhaps that's why, when the time comes to say *enough of this horror*, it is someone other than the alcoholic who is the first to do so. After all, the addict himself is immersed in denial due to his fear of reality and that denial is reinforced by the numbing effect of the drugs he uses. At any rate, it is frequently the non-addicted loved ones who walk through the therapist's door tearfully announcing their life has become unmanageable and isn't there something we can do to make him stop drinking?

Right off, keeping in mind there is no law prohibiting the consumption of alcohol by adults over the age of 21, let's answer that two-part question. Here's the good news and the bad news in that order. (1) There's something you can do. (2)

It probably won't make the alcoholic stop drinking. Besides, it's been established already that stopping drinking doesn't solve the problem, so it's in everyone's best interest to stop talking as though it will. Too much disillusionment and heartbreak result from the f alse hope that quitting is all it takes. And although an individual alcoholic can't get well until he stops drinking, something more far-reaching is needed.

Everyone needs to change.

We've isolated that statement on the page for several reasons. The first is to emphasize the concept as being at the very heart of recovery. It reminds us that there is no such thing as overcoming addiction without major changes. What must change is more than just the alcoholic's drinking habit. Alcoholism is a lifestyle, a personality configuration and a view of the world. It embraces the whole person to such an extent that the addict who is healed will be virtually unrecognizable to those who knew him *way back when*. Without these kinds of changes, the alcoholic will surely relapse.

A second important point of emphasis is with the word *everyone*. It is not only the alcoholic who must change. If we seem to return to this idea many times over, doing so speaks to how important it is. We repeat it for fear someone might miss it and if we forget that the addict's loved ones (especially his family) are a part of the alcoholism, we should expect nothing less than relapse.

Family members must change. This doesn't mean the addict's recovery is the responsibility of his family. Always, he must make choices and assume responsibilities. Nevertheless, the family doesn't need his alcoholism or even his presence in order to be an alcoholic family. He could leave forever and unless those left behind make changes, they will be an alcoholic family forever.

Finally there's the word itself. When it comes to addiction, *change* is not a transitive verb. That is, individuals change; they do not change others. In fact, one of the wildest delusions concocted by the ego of man is the idea that one person is capable of overriding the will of another and making him do something he doesn't choose to do. One's free will is a gift of God and is required if we're to have a relationship with Him. Without our will and the freedom to reject God's love, we would not have the freedom to accept it. We would be automatons, less than human machinery, incapable of entering into friendship with Him. Even God does not deprive us of that freedom. He could have stopped Adam from disobeying. But He didn't. It's presumptuous of us to think we should or even can.

The first change to be made is that each concerned family member needs to stop trying to change anyone else, especially the addict. Leave him alone. As for the rest, leave each other alone. Take your cue from Jesus who said to turn your attention to the plank in your own eye.

If the family has an impact on the alcoholic's continued drinking, it will not be through cajoling, manipulation, threats, bribes, or trickery. If the alcoholic changes, it will be because his family has surrounded him with an atmosphere of wellness and as the chapters on codependency and adult children of alcoholics demonstrate, wellness hasn't been the order of the day up until now.

The next step is to dispense with the three rules, beginning with *don't talk*. Someone must take the initiative by speaking up about the elephant in the room. This person can call a meeting of everyone with the exception of the addict. At this point neither the addict nor anyone else is ready to deal with the alcoholic circus that will result from such a premature confrontation. The purpose at this time is to name the elephant. Its name is *Alcoholism*. Refuse to call it anything else.

Let's Have an Intervention

Intervention is a technique of somewhat fleeting popularity and dubious effectiveness which has been utilized to pressure active addicts into entering treatment. The very existence of interventions indicates the reluctance of the addict to seek help, usually because he is in denial or he just doesn't wish to abandon his current lifestyle.

Using family members and other significant persons in the addict's life, all of whom have been rehearsed in advance, the addict is confronted about his behavior and given some sort of ultimatum. The addict is left with a choice between entering the treatment program which has been pre-selected for him or evoking the displeasure of everyone who has gone to such lengths to help him.

Setting up the intervention is a lot like producing a play. There is a director (usually a therapist) who casts the production with an eye to selecting those persons who will be appropriate and effective. A script is written in which each member of the cast prepares a persuasive speech to be read to the addict who will be brought to the intervention under the pretence he is being taken somewhere else, perhaps to a party. He is not informed in advance what is happening, because if he knew what's going on, he wouldn't show up. When the team is sufficiently rehearsed, they gather to await the arrival of the unsuspecting addict and his escort. When they arrive, after an awkward transition away from *let's have a party*, the intervention begins.

We see several problems here. First of all, the process begins by deceiving the addict -- employing the sort of manipulation everyone decries as unacceptable whenever the alcoholic does the same thing. Secondly, the process focuses on one individual – the active addict – and leaves the rest of the family thinking that the problem resides with him alone and that getting him into treatment will solve their problem. Thirdly, the undertaking is a setup for the addict to cry *foul* when he convinces himself he's been victimized. Which he most certainly will. Fourth, the process of eliminating participants who are considered unsuited for the intervention may create a rift in the family and undermine the healing process. Lastly, the need to choose team members from the immediate family increases the likelihood that one or more of them may be in such denial that their participation sabotages the project from within.

Failure to see these issues is a failure to understand that addiction is a family matter. *If the blind lead the blind, then both shall fall in the ditch.*

That being said, let's return to the family meeting without the addict and to the task of creating an atmosphere of wellness to draw the alcoholic toward recovery. This will be a more realistic sort of intervention. An environment in which normal people live is one in which wellness thrives. Let us recall the observations made in Chapter VI. We said normal is one of those hard to define words that everyone knows what he means when he says it, but no one can tell you what it means exactly. We noted two other words that fall into this category -- *okay* and *appropriate*. Our definition of normal is a composite of all three. Normal is what most people consider appropriate and okay. Conversely, if most people say something is inappropriate and not okay, then it isn't normal. Now let's revisit the five indicators of the normal life identified earlier.

(1) *Intoxication.* Item number one concerns alcohol consumption. Because the presence of alcohol or other addictive substances exert such subtle influences upon the psyches of persons in addiction, it may be difficult for some of us to grasp the reality of the influence. Nevertheless, addicts in early recovery are so prone to preoccupation with alcohol that just being exposed to it is enough to set off a thought process that leads to relapse and the potential processes are so numerous that it is virtually impossible to address each one in advance of it's occurrence. At the very least, this preoccupation will slow the growth process the addict must experience to achieve sobriety. The same pressures apply to the entire family, because each of them has incorporated patterns of thinking, feeling and acting which are characteristically alcoholic. For better or for worse the alcoholic family is a network of influences and in most cases the influence is *for worse.*

Here's just one example. A middle-aged couple with two sons were in a family session which was part of the elder, 23 year-old son's counseling for opiate addiction. Numerous rules had been established to secure his recovery, including complete abstinence, attendance at support groups, structured living, curfews and accountability. During the session the young man complained that none of the rules were being applied to his 18 year old brother who was allowed to come and go as he pleased with no accountability and regularly drank beer in the house with his parents' approval.

The father of the boys explained that it wouldn't be fair to the younger son to impose limits on him just because his older brother had a problem. Besides; he said the younger son knew his brother had enjoyed those same freedoms when he was 18 and that would make him angry. This was spoken by an intelligent, well educated, church attending husband and father from an upscale, enriched environment. He was also an ACOA. And after 50 years, man and boy, he thought more like a drug addict than his own, addicted son.

Hope for wellness requires that the family members be of one accord. If the family agrees that abstinence is essential to the wellness of the alcoholic in their midst, then they will need to agree to quit drinking themselves. Listen carefully after this proposal is made. If there are dissenters, there may be other addicts among you. If this is not the case, it may help to understand that often the most innocuous, drinking behavior will encourage the alcoholic to go on drinking. He's always happy to join in. It needs to be clear to him that he is the only one in the family who drinks – ever.

And the alcoholic family in recovery can no more abide the presence of alcohol than can the alcoholic himself.

Why should we give up our harmless pleasure just because one of us can't handle it? First of all, anyone who's been paying attention can attest that in a family such as this, drinking is never harmless; and secondly, that's what normal families do. They make sacrifices. b*ut I don't even live in the same house with him. How's he going to know?* He'll know. And some day when he's sober, he'll thank you.

(2) *Abuse.* The second item on the agenda is the matter of hurting one another. It's not possible to identify every occasion with potential for abusive treatment of one another, but it's a reasonable guess that a lot of repressed resentment, grief and anxiety have been bubbling to the surface on a regular basis. In fact, this will probably require counseling to resolve the issues that developed between members over the years. The sooner the family gets into counseling, the better. This calls for a specialized type of counseling provided by an addictions specialist experienced in working with the families of addicts. With all due respect to the gifted, excellent licensed marriage and family counselors out there, many of whom are hopefully reading this, this is not the time for that sort of counseling.

(3) *Manipulation.* Regarding the matter of manipulating one another; a practice stemming from viewing one another as opponents rather than sources of help and support, we reference the aforementioned call to sacrifice. Although it probably won't come easily, the goal is to replace the question *what can I get from you?* with the question *how can I help?* More counseling here.

When the name of the game is *manipulation,* like all games there is an objective and a set of rules and procedures. The objective of the game is to get one's opponent to voluntarily do something that he doesn't wish to do. Immediately we identify other family members as opponents which is antithetical to the concept of family. As for the rules of the game, there are none other than the one stating the end (winning) justifies the means. The game is played by employing whatever means will deceive or pressure one's opponent into believing that it's to his advantage to do what in reality is a violation of his personality and integrity. Obviously, this calls for dishonesty which invariably undermines sobriety and family bonds.

(4) *Dishonesty.* Here comes a really big one. Make it a practice to speak only the truth.

(5) *Isolation.* Lastly, seek out every opportunity to spend time together. Eat meals together. Go to church together. Do household chores together. Watch television together. Read aloud to one another. Take walks together. Play together. Pray together. And go ahead and break that old rule together. Talk! In all cases, and especially in this one, don't let the alcoholic set the tone. The alcoholic (the elephant in the room) has so powerfully dominated the household with his presence, that the family has been accommodating him for years. This will need to change.

The addict himself ought not to be excluded from family activities, but any disruptive, alcoholic behavior should be put on *extinction*. Putting behavior on extinction means refusing to respond to it at all. Without reinforcement of any sort, a behavior will eventually extinguish itself like a fire no one fuels. (It should go without saying that dangerous or life threatening behavior must never be ignored.)

What needs to change most is the identity of each family member. The enabling *Director of Operations,* the excellent *Public Relations* person, the troublesome *Prodigal,* the *Misfit* and the *Entertainer:* each one of them must quit his job. In order to accomplish this the belief system governing our lives must change. Recalling the paradigm outlined in prior chapters, each member must discover his central belief system that generates distorted thinking, painful feelings and ungodly decision making.

The descriptions of the identities and their emotional states set down in Chapter VI may help point to the false beliefs that probably give rise to the various personalities. Each must discover his true identity in Christ through the therapeutic methods that were developed in the preceding chapters.

What if, after all this work, this person you alternately love and wish to strangle keeps right on drinking? What if he doesn't change? Oh, he'll change. He's alcoholic, not stupid. He'll realize the family system he used to control has ceased to respond to his manipulation. He'll know you don't require a drunk at the center of your lives anymore and that you want him restored to his family as God intended. If you persevere and not grow faint, in time he'll know you've changed for good. While you're waiting for your miracle, take a look at yourselves and at one another. You'll see what a normal, happy family you've become.

One day you and your loved one will smile when he says, *I don't drink anymore. I decided there's no future in it.* In that moment, recall the words set down centuries ago by the prophet, Jeremiah. They are the words of the one who holds the future.

I know the plans I have for you, plans to prosper you and not to harm you, plans to give you hope and a future.

May you find Him now.

EIGHT

Neuroscience

For Brainy Types

We begin this chapter with an apology to the dedicated and highly talented researchers in the field of neuropsychology for whom what follows will be a gross over simplification. We offer this disclaimer with the greatest of admiration and appreciation for the work being done in the field. Our modest hope is that by scratching the surface, we may provide some rudimentary insights into what goes on inside the skulls of addicts as well as the rest of us not so brainy types.

Neuroscience includes the study of the anatomy and physiology of the nervous system and our main concern here is the human brain. Right off we're barging into the most complicated aspect of neuroscientific study. Human behavior involves so many variables that it could take forever to unravel the intricate network of causes and effects that occur in the brain. We get an idea of the complexity of the subject when we note that no one knows how many neurons (brain cells) are present in the human nervous system but estimates range between billions and a trillion. Anyone interested in counting them may wish to know that if one person counted one neuron per second, counting a billion neurons would take one individual more than 31years if he counted day and night non-stop without so much as a single naptime or potty break. If he wants to keep counting to the trillion mark, he'll need to reserve 31,000 years on his Day-timer.

Distinguishing anatomy and physiology as studies of structure and function of organisms in that respective order brings us to the question of mind versus matter. Traditionally persons called *dualists* have taken the position that mind and matter -- matter being the observable materials comprising the nervous system -- are separate entities. Identifying the brain as separate from the mind readily accommodates the idea that there is a spiritual entity which survives decomposition.

On the other hand, the *monists* view the mind to be the function of the nervous system. If people were automobiles, the engine would be the brain and the movement of the car when the brain is in operation would be the mind. Following this line of thinking, one concludes that when there's no brain, there's no mind just as there's no movement when the engine is disabled. The position of neuroscience appears to be with the monists. Setting aside any urge toward a theological confab, it is reasonable to remember that along side the idea expressed as *mind over matter* we often hear the one about a *sound mind in a sound body.* Therefore, our interest in neuroscience is an interest in how the brain is structured, how it operates and most important for the alcoholic, what happens to the mind of a drunk when he tampers with the delicate chemistry of the central nervous system.

That brings us to chemistry. When the brain is working, it is undergoing multiple chemical interactions and the process requires a proper balance of the elements and compounds involved. For this reason, there is a protective wall called the blood-brain barrier which surrounds the blood vessels of the brain to prevent elements circulating in the bloodstream that would disrupt brain function from reaching the neurons within. However, the barrier is semipermeable which means that some substances are able to get through. Yes -- you guessed it -- among those substances are alcohol and certain other intoxicants.

The downside of all this is that you get to poison your mind. On the upside you can medicate your mind after you've poisoned it. We'd like to interject, however, that self-medication is just as bad an idea as is poisoning yourself and that any corrective steps should be taken under the direction of a properly trained and licensed physician. Ideally that physician ought to be a board certified psychiatrist.

Before proceeding, let's look at the structure of the basic neuron, or what some people call a brain cell. Not all brain cells are the same. They vary according to the jobs they do. However, they have four basic parts in common which are shown in the drawing which follows.

The four parts of the neuron are:

> *1. soma:* the body of the cell which contains the nucleus and its operating system.
>
> *2. dendrites :*extensions through which signals from other cells are received across a space between the terminal button and the dendrite called the *synapse*.
>
> *3. axon:* an extension which carries the signal from the body of the cell to the terminal buttons.
>
> *4. terminal buttons:* points from which a chemical called a neurotransmitter is released to carry a signal (or message) across the synapse to the next cell.

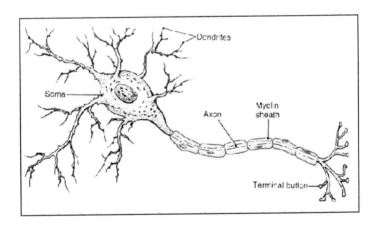

Basic Neuron Structure

Ultimately our focus will be upon the neurotransmitter, because regulation (or deregulation) of these chemicals can be the genesis of physical addiction. Invasive substances crossing the blood-brain barrier and affecting the neurotransmitters can be the substances referred to in the expression *substance dependence.*

Within the individual neuron there is a movement of ions in and out of the cell which creates an electrical impulse which travels along the axon until it reaches the terminal buttons. At this point a neurotransmitter is released which facilitates the communication of the 'message' to another cell which is part of a sequence. When neurons interact with one another, they produce certain behaviors. For our purposes we are applying the term behavior not just to observable movement, but all human conduct including what we usually refer to as thinking and feeling. The way in which much of this is accomplished remains a mystery, but research into the subject continues. Action, for want of a better word, exists first in the individual cell.

How does a specific behavioral process look on a cellular level? Although neuroscientific concerns related to addiction are focused upon cellular activity within the brain, a simpler, more easily understood example of neural communication is in the reflex response which takes place in the peripheral nervous system. This involves what happens when a person touches a dangerously hot object. A sensory neuron in the hand that touches a hot stove is excited and sends the impulse (action potential) along its axon which terminates in the spinal cord. By way of a neurotransmitter, the impulse excites the receptors of a second neuron which transmits the impulse to a motor neuron which sends the impulse along its axon to where it meets with a nerve that connects to a muscle. At the terminal buttons of the motor neuron, the excitatory impulse is transmitted to the muscle and causes it to contract and the hand is withdrawn from the hot stove.

Clearly this simple, neural transmission is nevertheless complicated enough for us to agree that it depends upon precision accuracy, especially since the entire process is taking place in a split second. Imagine the result if the chemistry involved were disrupted so that the action potential were inhibited rather than excited. There would be considerable weeping and wailing and gnashing and howling and hopping. All of that would require even more neural activity.

Earlier references to *synapses* re mind us that they play an essential role in neural communication. Synapses are points of connection between the terminal buttons of one cell and the receptors of another. The neurotransmitter released by the terminal button into the synaptic cleft (the space between cells) ensures the signal will move from cell to cell and that it will have either an excitatory or an inhibitory effect upon the cell which receives the message. Admittedly an oversimplification, it's as though one cell is telling another to speed up or slow down or perhaps to go or to stop. Whether the process excites or inhibits is determined by the receptors and which elements they permit to enter or leave the cell.

Once the action is complete, any residual transmitter left in the synaptic cleft is either destroyed or returned to the sending neuron. This latter process is called reuptake. When reuptake is delayed or prevented for some reason, the result may be a prolongation or intensification of the effect. We can track this process in the drawing of a terminal button and a receptor membrane which follows.

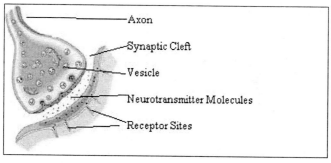

Terminal Button and Synapse

The action impulse moves along the axon membrane to the terminal button containing vesicles in which the neurotransmitter is stored. The impulse causes the vesicles to release the neurotransmitter particles into the synaptic cleft where they defuse until they contact the post-synaptic membrane containing receptors. Certain receptors bind with certain transmitters and there must be a proper fit to allow the appropriate impulse to pass to the adjacent neuron. We will see later that some drugs and medications which have crossed the blood-brain barrier from other sources may also bind (connect) with certain receptors so that the transmission and the resultant behaviors may be positively or negatively affected by these intruders.

Just how important is the synapse? Without what happens in the synapse, one of two disasters would result. Each action potential would dead-end at a terminal button and that would be all she wrote; or every action potential would rush off willy-nilly in all directions causing utter, cognitive chaos. Regarding the first, the organism would die, because the impulses (messages) that tell the heart to beat and the lungs to breathe would wind up in the dead letter office. With the second, imagine a network of railroad tracks in a freight yard with no brakemen or switchmen to control the movement of the cars. In order to bring order to the whole neurological system, there must be a system of traffic control.

How is that control accomplished? Basically what determines whether an action potential is passed on to another neuron is the presence of a receptor which is compatible with the neurotransmitter which was released by the presynaptic neuron. Imagine the receptor to be like a household electrical outlet and the neurotransmitter to be represented by the plug on a lamp. Further refine the analogy by saying there are many different shapes and sizes of plugs and outlets, and only when the two are matched up can the connection be made and the light be turned on.

A more contemporary analogy for this system may be seen in the way a desktop computer is connected with it's attachments. Wires run from the main computer box to the printer, the mouse, audio speakers, keyboard and so on. The connectors on each end of the wires have different shapes and designs and they match their receptacles so that the printer cannot accidentally be connected to the keyboard or the mouse. In this way only the signals intended for the printer can reach the printer.

Commonly identified neurotransmitters include:

1.   *Acetylcholine:*   provides   for   the communication of impulses that cause muscle contraction. Interference with the release of this neurotransmitter can result in paralysis.

2.   *Dopamine*:   studies suggest that it is also involved in movement, as well as the ability to maintain focus and in the processes of learning. Most important for our purposes, it appears to be connected to responses that reinforce the use of drugs that are addictive.

3.   *Norepinephrine:* this transmitter produces elevated   levels   of   attentiveness   and vigilance.

3.   *Serotonin:* the effects of serotonin are various. Relative to addiction, it affects mood and appears to be involved in regulating pain. Many antidepressant medications are designed to inhibit the reuptake of serotonin.

4.   *Glutatamate:* both glutatamate and GABA affect the degree of excitation and regulate the speed at which action potentials occur. Alcohol, among other drugs, affects glutamate.

5.   *Gamma-aminobutyric acid (GABA):* this is the most inhibiting neurotransmitter in the brain and perhaps the most significant when it comes to addiction. Inhibition ensures stability in the brain because without it cells in the network would create chaos with their random firing. GABA receptors also bind with benzodiazepines, barbiturates and ethyl alcohol.

Each of these carries an impulse from its neuron of origin and binds only with receptors in adjacent cells which are compatible with it.

Certain drugs which include benzodiazepines, commonly referred to as tranquilizers, along with barbiturates and alcohol are all able to cross the blood-brain barrier and find their way to post synaptic receptors which ordinarily bind with GABA (gamma-amniobutyric acid) transmitters. How then, does physical addiction to these drugs take place?

Well, some call it laziness while others see it as a proclivity for the conservation of energy, but any way you call it, it seems to be a characteristic of human nature to avoid excess work. Apparently this trait applies to neurons as well, for when drugs that bind to certain *feel good* receptors are introduced externally, (drinking, eating, injecting, inhaling) the neuron may stop producing its own transmitters and rely on the drug instead. When the drug is removed, that is, when the user goes off it cold turkey, not only is he without the drug, the neurons have ceased to supply necessary transmitters. Thus he experiences withdrawal, which is a fairly accurate indicator of physiological addiction.

This explains why withdrawal symptoms are opposite to the effects produced by the neurotransmitter or its exogenous replacement. When the transmitter isn't being synthesized and the substitute drug has been removed, then the appropriate impulse isn't received. If the message was supposed to say *relax*, the system remains tense.

The reasons why the individual is using the drug in the first place may be many and complex and certain of those motives may be related to characterological issues. However our purpose here is to concentrate on neuron function as it relates to physical addiction. Relative to that, certain individuals may be drawn to drug use due to a congenital abnormality affecting the regulation of neurotransmitters and their receptors. For such individuals who seem never to have felt *okay* inside themselves, the discovery of alcohol or some drug that binds with GABA receptors seems like an answer to a lifetime of prayer. Looking back on early experiences, some addicts recall thinking during their first encounter with alcohol that *this is the way I want to feel for the rest of my life!* Such reports support the argument that addicts are born that way, although this is not always the case.

Now, before we get too comfortable with this information and the thought that that's all there is and *now I get it,* let's remind ourselves that if anything were that simple, we wouldn't need billions of cells to work our brains.

In addition to aforementioned personality factors, in some instances the intruder substance is not one that replaces neurotransmitters (agonist) but rather one that blocks the reuptake process (reuptake inhibitor) so that the synaptic cleft is flooded and the postsynaptic receptors are overloaded. For the addict this is great while it lasts, but this *party in your skull* puts the brain to work shutting down receptor sites in order to restore a normal balance. Sooner or later the *candyman* takes a day off and the individual finds himself with half his receptors boarded up and no way to process the normal supply of transmitters. Again we have withdrawal, but this time it's on the other side of the synaptic cleft. In either case, the result may be physical dependence.

We've been throwing around terms like some annoying name-dropper -- terms like *agonist* and *reuptake inhibitor* -- and we better take time to clarify a few before the reader decides to use these pages for tinder. We'll take a quick look at some neuroscientific jargonese; mainly drugs or medications classified according to the way they affect neural transmission.

1. *Reuptake Inhibitor:* commonly abbreviated according to the neurotransmitter they affect (SSRI or Selective Serotonin Reuptake Inhibitor) this substance blocks reuptake and extends the time a transmitter remains in the synaptic cleft.

2. *Antagonist:* keeps a receptor from being activated. There are several ways in which this may be accomplished, but the bottom line is prevention of appropriate response.

3. *Agonist:* any substance that binds to a receptor and activates it or makes it easier for the neurotransmitter to bind. Either way, the receptor is more likely to be activated. The agonist is not the neurotransmitter but it produces a similar effect.

4. *Partial Agonist:* similar to agonists in that it binds with a receptor but doesn't produce as intense an impulse as the actual transmitter would. In situations where excessive transmitters are being released, (schizophrenia) a partial agonist may prove an effective intervention in modulating responses.

Anybody Who Goes to a Psychiatrist Ought to Have His Head Examined!

Keep in mind that Alcoholics Anonymous is only about 70 years old and that when we use the phrase, *back in the old days*, it wasn't very long ago. Members looked upon as old-timers might only have had a few years of sobriety. Nevertheless, the old-timers then as the old-timers today were listened to and revered by new-comers hoping to find sobriety themselves. Well, back in the old days the sentiment expressed in the subtitle above was heard more often than it is today in the rooms of AA but occasionally we still hear it. When it surfaces it harks back to the simple belief that alcohol is a drug and psychiatrists give you drugs. What sort of insanity must it require to give drugs to someone trying to get off drugs?

For years a kind of civil war raged between the docs and the old-timers, each hoping to defeat the common enemy and disagreeing upon methods, especially when it came to administering medication. Incidentally, without question an addict can go into such severe withdrawal that he may die without proper medication. Back in the old days the only available medication for alcohol withdrawal was more alcohol. Go figure.

How can the findings of neuroscience help to resolve this conflict? The answer lies in the fact that some medications are hazardous to recovery and others are not. First, it appears that the probability of developing a dependence on a drug is directly proportionate to the length of time it acts upon (and in) the brain. The stimulant, methylphenidate (Ritalin) contrasts with cocaine in this respect and the development of methadone to combat heroin dependence relies upon this factor. However, protracted abuse of methadone or methylphenidate has also been known to lead to dependence.

Selective Serotonin Reuptake Inhibitors (SSRI) are long acting and they don't seem to affect the synthesis or the release of serotonin. Instead, they prolong its presence in the synaptic cleft without seeming to disrupt the chemical composition within the cells. Without changes affecting transmission and reception, dependence is not likely. The SSRI's effectiveness as a mood elevator is contingent upon the ability of the neuron to produce serotonin in the first place. If an SSRI is given to a depressed person whose serotonin production has been limited due to cell damage from drug abuse, he will remain depressed. Then his condition sends him looking for an exogenous substitute. Ironically, he may choose alcohol which tends to deepen depression that will be followed by anxiety during withdrawal.

Cocaine

How odd that we've come this far without mentioning cocaine. Let's say we've been saving the worst for last. We did link it with methylphenidate just a few paragraphs back to make the point that one is less of a problem than the other. Both are reuptake inhibitors, so why isn't cocaine a proper antidepressant or a therapeutically appropriate stimulant? Well, there's much more to cocaine than just that. Talk about a party in your head! Cocaine serves up a virtual smorgasbord of neural activity. First and foremost it blocks the reuptake of dopamine. Evidence also suggests it's a norepinephrine reuptake inhibitor, a serotonin reuptake inhibitor, an opioid agonist, an NMDA receptor agonist, a sodium channel block and it stimulates the release of dopamine into the synaptic cleft. Wait there may be more.

Oh, yes. Cocaine's effect upon dopamine, which is to block reuptake of that neurotransmitter is apparently responsible for heightened levels of pleasure which dopamine produces. There's nothing like pleasure to reinforce the behavior that brought it on and when the behavior is snorting a line, well, you know.

This just in: research points to the likelihood that the connection between dopamine and pleasure is that the dopamine release (rush) is tied to the surprise we get when an experience turns out to be more pleasant than expected. Hand an infant a cup of Coca-Cola when he expects tepid water and the neurons spit out the dopamine with the message, *this is greeeaaat!* Watch him eagerly reach for more when he gets the message. Now try the same thing with an adult. Put crack cocaine in his pipe when he's expecting tobacco, and watch him light up. Remember, pleasure is the great reinforcer.

Drugs like benzodiazepines; ie, Xanax are especially threatening to recovery from addiction because unlike reuptake inhibitors, they bind with, let us say a GABA receptor, even though there's not a speck of GABA within 30 miles of the synapse. The fact that the source of the Xanax is external means the amount of the "dose" is not subject to internal, neural regulation and in nearly all cases its presence becomes disruptive. It's like souping up a car engine with an octane level fuel it can't tolerate.

This potential for mismanagement reminds us of the earlier assertion that there's a fine line between medicating and poisoning the mind. That which is introduced into the brain should be overseen by a licensed psychiatrist.

What Ever Happened to Charlie?

Before we lower the curtain on this glimpse *Beyond Denial,* let's have one last look at John's story of Charlie the cripple which we recounted in Chapter One. We'll return to the point where Jesus told Charlie to get up. John says:

At once the man was cured; he picked up his mat and walked.

Perhaps, in light of today's accumulated knowledge, one might say it another way.

"A neuron was stimulated in Charlie's brain and positively charged sodium ions passed through the protective cell membrane and at that moment an action potential was born! The newly created electrical impulse hurried along the axon membrane until it reached the terminal buttons of Charlie's neuron. Openings in the cell membrane closed behind the sodium ions to await the next impulse.

"Meanwhile, arriving at the terminal button, the action potential encountered a synapse just beyond which lay a cleft like a forbidding castle moat ensuring that the electrical impulse would not invade the adjacent cell. Would this be the end of all hope that Charlie would ever walk again?

"Not to worry. The impulse from the presynaptic neuron triggered the release of its trusty neurotransmitters which were safely hidden inside vesicles in the terminal buttons ready for such an emergency. Out poured the transmitters into the synaptic cleft, spreading out until they reached the other side where they came upon the membrane of a dendrite on a receiving neuron.

"As the transmitters, like special forces personnel emerging into the light of a fire fight collided with the membrane, they bound with the receptors on the far side. Each receptor was excited by the impulse that was the action potential. The sequential exchanges continued, moving from neuron to neuron until the message reached the spinal cord, the peripheral nervous system and the extensor muscles of Charlie's legs. Motor neurons picked up the message, and the muscles began to contract; and then -- Charlie began to walk!"

Now how's that for a miracle? But we're still left with one, puzzling, disconcerting and unanswered question: *Who started all this movement in the first place?*

May you find Him now.